"What an invaluabying to
do it all: leading th                                      people
amid the ups and d<                                       haddix
provide explicit bibl                                 ... y pastor
who wants to do all or the above with faithfulness, joy, and love for God and
the people he calls us to lead."

> **David Platt,** Pastor, McLean Bible Church, McLean, Virginia; Founder,
> Radical; author, *Don't Hold Back*

"In *Expositional Leadership*, Jim Shaddix and Scott Pace combine experienced
pastoring with years of training others for the pastorate to give insight into
how the ministry of the word contributes to the fulfillment of the local church's
leadership, preaching, and pastoring responsibilities. This needed book shows
how congregational ministry empowers the pulpit and how faithful pulpit
ministry is integral to congregational leadership and health. What many only
discover from decades of ministry is captured and treasured here."

> **Bryan Chapell,** pastor; author, *Christ-Centered Preaching*

"What a timely and much-needed work. I do not know of another book like
it. Bringing together in beautiful balance the work of leading, pastoring, and
preaching, Pace and Shaddix show us how we can fulfill our holy assignment
with integrity, competence, and joy."

> **Daniel L. Akin,** President, Southeastern Baptist Theological Seminary

"The sermon is by far the pastor's most influential leadership opportunity. In
*Expositional Leadership*, Scott Pace and Jim Shaddix demonstrate how preachers can steward that opportunity in a manner that is spiritually beneficial to
the congregation and consistent with the biblical calling of the pastor-teacher.
This rewarding book is, in equal parts, a pastoral theology, a biblical rationale
for expository preaching, and a solid philosophy of church leadership. *Expositional Leadership* offers valuable guidance for both the beginner pastor and
the experienced leader."

> **Stephen Rummage,** Senior Pastor, Quail Springs Baptist Church,
> Oklahoma City; Professor of Preaching and Pastoral Ministry,
> Midwestern Baptist Theological Seminary; author, *Planning Your
> Preaching*

"A biographer once said of John Calvin that the hardworking pastor and theologian assumed his whole ministerial labor was all about the exposition of Scripture. Everything centered on and flowed from exposition. In a similar spirit, Pace and Shaddix demonstrate how the numerous facets of pastoral ministry can and should be integrated by such a commitment. *Expositional Leadership* offers a model of pastoral ministry that allows the word of God to be the primary way a preacher leads, loves, and feeds the church. While there are many books on church leadership, homiletics, and pastoring, there aren't many that demonstrate how all three should work together. I highly recommend this book and plan on using it in future events and courses."

**Tony Merida,** Pastor for Preaching and Vision, Imago Dei Church, Raleigh, North Carolina; author, *The Christ-Centered Expositor*

"*Expositional Leadership* presents a threefold approach to pastoring, teaching, and preaching wherein leadership and pastoring are servants of preaching—not masters. This volume reenergizes leaders to respond to the actual needs of the church's present-day challenges with powerful tools, and it does so without compromising the integrity of the eternal word or diminishing its authority. Jim Shaddix and Scott Pace's *Expositional Leadership* is a book whose time has come for those dedicated to efficient and effective kingdom work."

**Robert Smith Jr.,** Charles T. Carter Baptist Chair of Divinity, Beeson Divinity School, Samford University

"Many books on preaching today wrongfully separate preaching from the primary call of a pastor to 'shepherd the flock of God that is among you' (1 Pet. 5:2). What we need are trusted voices to push against this trend and skillfully demonstrate how preaching is a primary task of the pastor's central calling. Pace and Shaddix are two of those voices. In *Expositional Leadership* they biblically and practically show how the preaching task is threaded through the shepherding call, not separated from it. Their insights are wise, helpful, and pastoral. Every pastor who desires to shepherd well through preaching should read this book."

**Brian Croft,** Founder and Executive Director, Practical Shepherding

*Expositional Leadership*

# Expositional Leadership

*Shepherding God's People from the Pulpit*

R. Scott Pace and Jim Shaddix

:: CROSSWAY®

WHEATON, ILLINOIS

*Expositional Leadership: Shepherding God's People from the Pulpit*
© 2024 by R. Scott Pace and Jim Shaddix
Published by Crossway
       1300 Crescent Street
       Wheaton, Illinois 60187

Cover image and design: Jordan Singer

First printing 2024

Printed in the United States of America

Trade paperback ISBN: 978-1-4335-8802-0
ePub ISBN: 978-1-4335-8805-1
PDF ISBN: 978-1-4335-8803-7

---

**Library of Congress Cataloging-in-Publication Data**

Names: Pace, R. Scott, author. | Shaddix, Jim, author.
Title: Expositional leadership : shepherding God's people from the pulpit / R. Scott Pace and Jim Shaddix.
Description: Wheaton, Illinois : Crossway, [2024] | Includes bibliographical references and index.
Identifiers: LCCN 2023001084 (print) | LCCN 2023001085 (ebook) | ISBN 9781433588020 (trade paperback) | ISBN 9781433588037 (pdf) | ISBN 9781433588051 (epub)
Subjects: LCSH: Christian leadership.
Classification: LCC BV652.1 .P323 2024 (print) | LCC BV652.1 (ebook) | DDC– 253dc23/eng/20230712
LC record available at https://lccn.loc.gov/2023001084
LC ebook record available at https://lccn.loc.gov/2023001085

---

Crossway is a publishing ministry of Good News Publishers.

| BP | | 33 | 32 | 31 | 30 | 29 | 28 | 27 | 26 | 25 | 24 |
|----|----|----|----|----|----|----|----|----|----|----|----|
| 15 | 14 | 13 | 12 | 11 | 10 | 9 | 8 | 7 | 6 | 5 | 4 | 3 | 2 | 1 |

# Contents

Introduction

# Leaders, Preachers, and Pastors

CHURCH LEADERSHIP IS CHALLENGING for a variety of reasons. Beneath the surface of a local church's culture is a complex history that can be difficult to see and assess. Every church body consists of people with various backgrounds, personalities, family situations, needs, and expectations. Often, there is also a wide range of spiritual maturity among members of the congregation that requires personal consideration and a versatile ministry approach. These challenges are compounded by the unforeseen circumstances and unexpected obstacles that pastors are constantly required to navigate as they attempt to lead the collective whole. Other pastors, as well as elders, administrative staff, and church leaders, can help shoulder some of the load, but leading a team and working with people creates additional dynamics that come with their own set of issues. In short, human beings are unpredictable, churches are complicated, and leadership is hard!

In addition to daily leadership challenges, pastors are always living under the pressure of the impending sermon. As soon as we step off the platform and emotionally exhale, the anticipation of the next message and the anxiety about its preparation begins to build. Even those of us who enjoy the process of sermon development recognize the ongoing mental and physical demands of preparing and preaching weekly messages (and sometimes more).

The sacred trust of delivering God's word is a sobering honor that we celebrate with gratitude and embrace with reverence. But if we're honest, the most difficult challenge related to preaching is not the never-ending process of sermon preparation or the unique blend of exhilaration and exhaustion that comes with delivering a message. It's the overwhelming disappointment we feel as we watch our people seemingly disregard the truth of God's word that we so desperately strive to communicate to them. Their lives continue to exhibit the same broken pieces and patterns, and the church body feels unmoved and unmotivated. Our initial misguided feelings of betrayal eventually give way to frustration and discouragement as we begin to struggle with doubts related to our preaching or with questions concerning our calling and our church. Preaching, as enjoyable as it is, can become a real struggle.

If leadership and preaching aren't difficult enough, the daily grind of pastoring can make ministry feel impossible and, on some days, miserable. The strain on our families, barrage of unrealistic expectations, constant demands on our time, spiritual weight of empathy for our people, and apparent lack of appreciation can absolutely debilitate even the most gifted pastor. Indeed, apart from God's sustaining grace and his supernatural strength, pastoral ministry is unbearable and unmanageable. As we struggle to persevere, we long to see God work in our congregants' lives and desperately pray for his fresh work in our own. These earnest desires, along with the constant demands, make pastoring both a humbling privilege and a heavy burden.

Overall, these three core components of our ministries—leadership, preaching, and pastoring—are all essential aspects of our calling. Although most of us recognize the inherent challenges that come with each of them (and certainly don't need a book to remind us), it's easy to overlook how interrelated and mutually dependent they are on one another. As a result, we can also fail to see how addressing them collectively can simplify their individual challenges. Most importantly, if we fail to recognize how Scripture weds leadership, preaching, and pastoring together, we may find ourselves attempting to fulfill each of their related responsibilities without actually accomplishing any of them.

## Surveying the Landscape

The unhealthy differentiation between leadership, preaching, and pastoring is also reflected in the broader landscape of contemporary ministry. In the same way that we compartmentalize these three core components of our calling, ministry resources typically address them separately as well. For example, leadership books often focus on principles and processes but rarely address practical aspects of pastoring. Similarly, pastoral resources provide helpful insights for our various roles and responsibilities but give little to no attention to preaching. And homiletics resources are designed to enhance our interpretation and communication skills, but they are largely silent on pastoral and leadership matters. While each of these subjects certainly warrant dedicated volumes, their artificial isolation and borderline exclusion of one another ignores the mutual dependence they share. This is one reason why expositional leadership is so important—it helps us integrate these foundational concepts.

But our segregation of these essential ministry components is not just theoretical—it's practical. In each of our ministries we all have responsibilities that require us to allocate time for sermon preparation, pastoral care and counseling, and organizational leadership (strategic scheduling is a must for every faithful pastor). Yet, some pastors may recognize preaching as a ministry strength and devote an unhealthy portion of their time to sermon development while they neglect pastoral care for the flock. Others may be gifted in the area of leadership and overemphasize vision and strategy to a point that it devalues people and sees them as an obstacle to overcome or a necessary evil to be put up with. Still others may not see themselves as gifted communicators and thus dedicate themselves to caring for the flock but minimize the amount of time spent in sermon preparation.

While we all have areas of strengths and weaknesses, and each of us has different passions and preferences, we must avoid concentrating on one core component of ministry at the expense of another. However, this is not simply a balance problem; it's also a blending problem. This is another reason why expositional leadership is crucial—it helps us determine how these core components of ministry overlap and how we can synthesize them together for maximum ministry impact.

Sadly, this unhealthy segregation of duties is not only obvious in our ministry approach and the related resources but is even more apparent in many ministry failures that occur. Pastors typically don't lose their churches because they suddenly adopt some errant doctrine or stumble into a moral failure. To be sure, these are not uncommon, but they are not the most frequent source of ministry collapse. Rather, pastors are dismissed and churches split over unwise and unhealthy leadership. Further, pastors often resign because churches can become riddled with internal turmoil due to a lack of spiritual maturity, which ultimately reflects an anemic preaching ministry. Likewise, when the people don't feel cared for and the sermons seem detached from their lives (no matter how exegetically accurate they are), a pastor can lose the trust and confidence of the congregation, forcing him to eventually leave.

When these types of situations begin to unravel, we find ourselves focusing on the symptoms instead of identifying and resolving the source of the problems. In other words, we point the hose at the smoke instead of the fire, which leaves the ministry in ashes, the people with scars, and the pastors severely burned. In each of these common scenarios, the failure in one core component leads to struggles in the others. But the opposite can also be true, and this is yet another reason why expositional leadership is critical. It helps us to leverage each component for the strength and success of the others, thereby solidifying and safeguarding our ministry.

### Establishing the Boundaries

As we explore the concept of expositional leadership it is important to establish some doctrinal and philosophical boundaries. These theological guardrails can keep us out of doctrinal ditches and also serve as guides that will steer our conversation in the right direction. There are several theological convictions and commitments that undergird our perspective and ultimately guide our approach. Each of these foundational truths feed and fuel the nature and necessity of expositional leadership.[1]

## God, Salvation, and the Church

We believe that the Creator of the universe is the one true, living, triune God who exists eternally in three persons—the Father, the Son, and the Spirit. He uniquely created people in his image (Gen. 1:26–27), but all of humanity was separated from him and condemned through Adam's original sin (Rom. 5:12). God's eternal plan of redemption was promised and pictured throughout the Old Testament (Gen. 3:15), and it was accomplished according to the Scriptures in the person and work of Christ the Son through his virgin birth, sinless life, substitutionary death on the cross, and bodily resurrection (1 Cor. 15:3–4). By faith, all those who repent and trust Christ as their Lord and Savior are personally and eternally saved (Rom. 10:9–10), adopted into God's family (1 John 3:1; Gal. 4:4–7), and established as new covenant members of Christ's body and bride, the church (Eph. 5:25–33). Believers are called to live and serve within a local community of faith that is conforming them, individually and collectively, into the likeness of the Son (Rom. 8:29; Eph. 4:12–16). Ultimately, as the fulfillment of God's redemptive plan, this life transformation is the goal of expositional leadership.

## The Sacred Scriptures

God has revealed his eternal nature and divine power through the magnitude and majesty of his creation (Rom. 1:20). More specifically, he has disclosed his personal nature through the living Word, Jesus (John 1:1–14; Heb. 1:3), and his written word, the Scriptures (Ps. 19:7–9; 2 Pet. 1:20–21). The Bible is the inspired, infallible, and inerrant word of God and therefore is sufficient as the sole and supreme authority of

---

1    In John Stott's classic *Between Two Worlds*, he sets forth five core convictions that establish the theological foundations for preaching. He argues that our homiletical approach will be determined by our convictions about God, Scripture, church, the pastorate, and preaching. John R. W. Stott, *Between Two Worlds: The Art of Preaching in the Twentieth Century* (Grand Rapids, MI: Eerdmans, 1982), 92–134.

everything that pertains to life, faith, and godliness (2 Tim. 3:16–17; 2 Pet. 1:3). Through the power and presence of God's Spirit, believers are able to understand and respond to the Scriptures (John 16:13; 1 Cor. 2:12–16). God's word is also the primary means by which his people are sanctified (John 17:17; 1 Pet. 2:2). Therefore, the word of God is the source and substance of expositional leadership.

## Pastoral Leadership

While God's people have equal worth and spiritual standing before the Lord, he has given leaders to the church to serve and equip his people (Eph. 4:11–12). In particular, he has established the office of pastor (or elder) within the church for those who are called and capable according to biblical qualifications (1 Tim. 3:1–7; Titus 1:5–9). As God's appointed undershepherds, pastors are called to serve Christ, the chief shepherd, by leading and feeding his people (1 Pet. 5:1–4; Acts 20:28). Pastors have stewardship responsibilities for the spiritual health of the church, bear a unique burden for God's people, and are called to exercise oversight in a loving and responsible manner (Heb. 13:17). These ordained responsibilities serve as the impetus for expositional leadership.

## Expository Preaching

A primary, and arguably the most important, responsibility of a pastor is to "preach the word" (2 Tim. 4:2). The success of his ministry will largely be measured by his faithfulness to teach the Scriptures accurately and effectively (2 Tim. 2:15). The preaching philosophy and practice that most faithfully honors the Bible as the word of God, allowing the text of Scripture to determine the substance and structure of the sermon, is exposition. This systematic approach, which regularly preaches through books or extended portions of the Bible, includes the clear explanation, application, and proclamation of a passage of Scripture. In other words, "Expository preaching is the process of laying open the biblical text in such a way that the Holy Spirit's intended meaning and accompanying power are brought to bear on the lives of contemporary listeners."[2] Since preaching is intended to be the central component of corporate worship and the Scriptures have the power to transform lives, the broadest congregational influence will occur when we preach to God's gathered people (1 Tim. 4:13–16; see Neh. 8:1–8). As a result, expository preaching is the model and the means by which expositional leadership is accomplished.

## Expositional Leadership

Based on these doctrinal convictions and the foundation they provide, we can establish the concept and core components of expositional leadership.

---

*Expositional leadership is the pastoral process of shepherding God's people through the faithful exposition of his word to conform them to the image of his Son by the power of his Spirit.*

---

Each component of this definition deserves a brief explanation.

- Expositional leadership is *pastoral* because preaching is the foundational and indispensable responsibility of those who are called to lead the church.
- Expositional leadership is a *process* because it is ongoing and continual. Leadership builds over time, not only in its leverage and influence but in its direction and progress.
- Expositional leadership involves *shepherding God's people* because it considers a particular context and congregation that must be led and fed according to their spiritual needs.
- Expositional leadership occurs *through the faithful exposition of God's word* because it requires the timeless truth of Scripture to be rightly interpreted and proclaimed.

2   Jerry Vines and Jim Shaddix, *Power in the Pulpit*, rev. ed. (Chicago: Moody, 2017), 30.

- Expositional leadership is intended to *conform the congregation to the image of God's Son* because its ultimate goal is the individual and corporate transformation of Christ's followers.
- Expositional leadership is only possible *by the power of his Spirit* because preaching for real heart transformation is utterly dependent on his supernatural work.

This working definition and its corresponding explanations provide the basis for our approach to expositional leadership in the chapters that follow. Each of the elements that comprise the definition are woven into various expressions of pastoral leadership through expository preaching.

### Charting the Course

Leadership is a multifaceted concept that includes various forms and functions, particularly within pastoral ministry. As we explore the concept of shepherding God's people through biblical exposition, there are six categories of leadership that can provide some structure to the conversation. Each chapter in this volume will focus on a specific aspect of pastoral leadership that can be leveraged through sermon development and delivery. The facets of leadership identified and discussed are not intended to be comprehensive, but, in our experience, they cover the most common (and essential) elements of pastoral leadership that should be employed through the faithful exposition of God's word.

The first chapter focuses on scriptural leadership. Here we aim to establish a biblical basis for a pastor's role in shepherding a congregation, the responsibilities it involves, the character and calling it requires, and the inseparable nature of expositional preaching and pastoral leadership. We will also consider how scriptural leadership must be distinguished from secular leadership in its form, function, and focus—otherwise, our preaching simply qualifies as motivational monologues, religious pep talks, or moralistic rants.

Chapter two explores the spiritual leadership that we should exert through our preaching. Ultimately, our faithful exposition is intended to result in spiritual transformation for us and for our congregations. Our ability to provide spiritual leadership depends on our own spiritual growth and maturity, which is enhanced through sermon development and expressed through sermon delivery. Beyond our own spiritual progress, a healthy pulpit ministry also determines the spiritual vitality and vibrancy of the church. In this chapter we explore how individual and corporate discipleship can be accomplished through the sermon and how biblical exposition equips our people to study Scripture in their own spiritual disciplines and devotion.

In the third chapter we address strategic leadership and how our messages should be designed for our specific contexts and congregations. Exposition should always be grounded in the authoritative meaning of the divine author as expressed through the biblical writer. This hermeneutical conviction and commitment guides our understanding of how the text can be pastorally applied in various churches. Yet, in order to effectively mobilize our congregations, we must also contextualize our messages for them as a distinct spiritual community. Through faithful exposition we can cast vision for our people and challenge them with congregational initiatives and collaborative efforts to accomplish God's mission and fulfill his will for our churches.

Servant leadership is the focus of chapter four. Here, we'll consider how to cultivate and establish a culture of humility and service among our people through text-driven preaching. This is not simply accomplished by preaching on servant-related passages, but is primarily achieved through our pulpit demeanor and preaching style. As pastors, we must demonstrate a Christlike humility through our sermon delivery as we exhort, challenge, plead, and compel our congregations according to the truth of the passage. Our disposition should display a love for our congregation and our community that models a compassion for people and motivates our members to live on mission with a servant mentality.

Chapter five focuses on situational leadership through our preaching ministry. Every church inevitably goes through difficult seasons of trial and hardship. These can be some of the most important times in the life of a church, and they require our careful consideration as we navigate them from the pulpit. People are looking for guidance and listening for truth that will anchor their hope in Christ, help them process circumstances through a biblical lens, and teach them how to respond accordingly. Whether it is a community tragedy or church crisis, we have the responsibility to preach with conviction and compassion as we shepherd our people through various situations with expositional messages.

The final chapter addresses sensible leadership in our preaching ministry. Too many churches have been damaged, too many ministries have been derailed, and too many pastors have been disqualified by the failure to exercise godly wisdom (and common sense) in preaching. Common pitfalls that seem obvious can actually become subtle traps that pastors fall into. As faithful preachers, we must avoid using our privilege to preach God's word on a soapbox by proclaiming our opinions, airing grievances, strong-arming the church, undermining others, or promoting ourselves. The pulpit is not a place for public arguments, political agendas, or personal ambition, so we must be careful to honor our calling and Christ's name through sensible leadership as his spokesmen.

Each of these six leadership concepts are essential to pastoral ministry and are best leveraged through our preaching ministries. They are practical areas that can help us weave leadership, preaching, and pastoring into a unified approach when guiding and feeding the congregations entrusted into our care. We pray that our journey together through *Expositional Leadership* will be one that deepens your walk and strengthens your work for our Savior!

1

# Scriptural Leadership from the Pulpit

*Until I come, devote yourself to the public reading*
*of Scripture, to exhortation, to teaching.*

1 TIMOTHY 4:13

THOSE OF US WHO CHAMPION expository preaching are sometimes asked whether the Bible mandates such a practice. We hear questions like, "Where in the Bible are we commanded to preach expositional sermons?" or "Can the sermons in the Bible that were preached by the prophets, Jesus, and the apostles legitimately be categorized as expository?" These are fair questions. The oversight in them, however, is the assumption that one of the reasons we have the Bible is to provide us with a homiletics textbook or a compilation of great sermons. The truth is, neither is the case. In fact, most of the "sermons" in the Bible are just fragments or summaries of sermons, and the number of texts that offer instructions on how to preach are few.

So where do we find a biblical foundation for expository preaching? We find it mostly in the way the Bible describes how preachers in the Old and New Testaments went about their tasks. For example, we learn in Nehemiah 8:1–12 that understanding and explaining Scripture is critical for the corporate gathering of God's people. We glean from Jeremiah 23:9–40 that God's prophets are responsible for being in his counsel to ensure that they say only what he says. We draw from Luke 4:16–21 that Jesus followed the rabbinic pattern in the synagogue of reading a passage from the Old Testament and then giving an exposition of it to the people, a pattern from which the apostles and the early church later took their cue.[1] And in 1 Corinthians, we see Paul describing himself as a "steward" of the gospel and refusing to compromise the message as he proclaimed the "testimony of God" (1 Cor. 2:1; 4:1). The common denominator in these representative passages is simply the responsibility of preachers to say—or uncover—what God says. That is exposition in its simplest form.

In addition to these descriptive references, the Bible also contains some imperatives regarding exposition. Peter says those with speaking gifts should "speak the oracles of God" (1 Pet. 4:11), and that certainly includes preachers. But maybe the most concise and direct command regarding exposition is Paul's instruction to Timothy: "Until I come, devote yourself to the public reading of Scripture, to exhortation, to teaching" (1 Tim. 4:13). This charge reveals the important relationship between leadership, exposition, and pastoral ministry. Paul weaves instruction about preaching together with Timothy's overall pastoral leadership, and he doesn't make much of a distinction between them. In fact, he appears to imply that Timothy's practice of public exposition of Scripture is the heart and the hinge of his leadership as a pastor.

The immediate context of this verse reinforces and further explains this interpretation. First Timothy 4:6–16 provides several critical principles involved in shepherding God's people from the pulpit, and each of these reveals some intersection between leadership, pastoral ministry, and biblical exposition. At their core, these principles are what makes expositional leadership scriptural. As we'll see from this passage, God's word is not only supposed to be the source and substance of our messages but also prescribes the attitude and approach that we, as pas-

---

1    John R. W. Stott, *Between Two Worlds: The Art of Preaching in the Twentieth Century* (Grand Rapids, MI: Eerdmans, 1982), 123.

tors, are supposed to embrace in order to lead God's people through the faithful exposition of his word.

## The Pastor's Motive Is the Master

The reason many pastors fail at being leaders is that they want to be leaders. While that may sound strange, we must understand that leadership is not the ultimate goal or standard of success when it comes to gospel ministry. The plethora of books, conferences, seminars, and courses on the subject of leadership feeds a misguided passion in many pastors simply because the world has touted it as a quality and skill of the highest order that's worthy of our greatest effort. Gospel leadership, however, is quite different. The Bible is clear that the way to be a good leader is not by developing skills to influence people and command organizations. Rather, the way to be a good leader is to be a good servant (Matt. 20:25–28; Mark 9:35).

Living according to this curious economy of leadership doesn't start with a focus on serving others—it begins with serving the Master who established that economy, the Lord Jesus Christ. The apostle Paul expects that his young protégé desires to be such a servant: "If you put these things before the brothers, you will be a good servant of Christ Jesus" (1 Tim. 4:6). Here, being a servant isn't described with the term that emphasizes submission and subjection as a slave (*doulos*), but the one used more generally for someone who serves another in some useful way (*diakonos*; see 1 Cor. 4:1–2; 2 Cor. 3:6; 6:4). Paul assumes that Timothy aspires to such a role in his relationship with Jesus. Thus, it must be the motive of every pastor not first to be a leader of people, but to be a useful servant of the Master. Leading people well will follow serving Jesus well.

But how does a pastor offer such useful service to our Lord? Though there are numerous ways this work plays out in gospel ministry, Paul lays out specific qualifications for being a "good servant" of the Master. And this is where pastoral leadership and biblical exposition begin to intersect in this passage. He first says that such servanthood will be realized "if you put these things before the brothers" (1 Tim. 4:6). Paul uses the term "these things" eight times in this letter to summarize the practical and doctrinal issues he's been addressing, things like prayer, modesty, authority and submission, qualifications of pastors and deacons, and destructive legalism.

Like Timothy, every pastor must lead his people to believe rightly and live obediently when it comes to all the aforementioned issues and more. That begins with "put[ting them] before" the congregation through preaching and teaching. The language Paul uses here conveys the idea of gentle persuasion through humble reminders—the pastor lovingly explains and applies God's word to his people so that they think rightly and live accordingly. Like a waiter, we serve our people nourishing meals; like a jeweler, we display before them treasured gems.[2] We are good servants of our Master if we lead well by preaching well.

Not only is the pastor a good servant when he preaches well but he preaches well because he learns well. Paul says Timothy's service for Christ and leadership of God's people intersect in his preaching ministry because he's been "trained in the words of the faith and of the good doctrine that [he has] followed" (1 Tim. 4:6). The idea of being trained is a metaphor for nurturing and tutoring children. Paul's use of the present participle suggests that his concern is for Timothy to continue feeding himself spiritually so that he can be a good servant of Jesus by training his congregation in the faith.[3]

So often we hear of pastors who neglect the study of God's word because of the many other pastoral responsibilities that demand their leadership. But studying God's word for spiritual nourishment and preaching preparation contributes directly toward pastoral leadership! We lead well when we preach well, and we preach well when we study and learn well. When a pastor regularly pursues his Master by digesting the truth of his word, consuming his gospel and feasting on his rich doctrine, then he can lead his people to "know how [they] ought

2   John R. W. Stott, *Guard the Truth: The Message of 1 Timothy and Titus*, The Bible Speaks Today (Downers Grove, IL: InterVarsity Press, 1996), 116.
3   Gordon D. Fee, *1 and 2 Timothy, Titus*, Understanding the Bible Commentary Series (Grand Rapids, MI: Baker Books, 2011), 103.

to behave in the household of God, which is the church of the living God, a pillar and buttress of the truth" (1 Tim. 3:15). Then and only then can he be considered a "good servant" of his Master.

## The Pastor's Goal Is Godliness

Leadership is not an end in and of itself; it naturally implies a destination. It's kind of like application and illustration in a sermon—these elements serve as means to other ends. We don't just do application in our sermons; we apply *something*. We use application to demonstrate how the truth is to be lived out. We don't just put illustrations in our sermons as rhetorical eye (or ear) candy; we put them in to illustrate *something*. We use them to either help us explain or apply the truth of the text. Neither application nor illustration stands alone in the sermon. We use them to accomplish greater purposes.

Christian leadership is often misunderstood in a similar way. It is not a stand-alone quality or characteristic in a pastor's life and ministry; it doesn't exist in a vacuum. Rather, it always involves a destination—we don't just lead, we lead *somewhere*. For Paul, that *somewhere* is godliness. He tells Timothy to "train [himself] for godliness" (1 Tim. 4:7), which, contrary to mere bodily exercise, "holds promise for the present life and also for the life to come" (1 Tim. 4:8). He assures the young pastor that such a pursuit is worth hard work and even suffering "because we have our hope set on the living God" (1 Tim. 4:10).

Overall, godliness is synonymous with being re-created into the *imago Dei*, the image of God in which humanity was originally made (Gen. 1:26–27). It's the godlikeness that was perverted, distorted, and aborted because of our sin but is now being restored in us through Christ's work. Thus, Paul tells Timothy to pursue this godliness for himself and his people because Jesus "is the Savior of all people, especially of those who believe" (1 Tim. 4:10). Godliness is made possible only through the gospel (Col. 3:10; Eph. 4:24).

This journey toward godliness begins at justification when our sins are forgiven, we're made right with God (Rom. 5:1), and his life is restored in us through the death and resurrection of Christ

(Rom. 5:8–10). The journey continues in the lifelong process of sanctification as we're made to look more and more like God through the work of Christ's Spirit in us (2 Cor. 3:18; 4:16). One day, this process will be completed in glorification when we finally and fully look like Christ at his return (1 John 3:1–3). The effectiveness of a pastor's leadership ability, then, must be measured by whether he's gradually moving himself and his people toward this destination. It doesn't matter what leadership abilities he possesses, the size of the church he pastors, or the breadth of his ministry platform. If he's not shepherding himself and his people to look more like Jesus, then he's not leading well when it comes to gospel ministry.

Practically speaking, this pursuit of godliness for ourselves and our people leads us to another intersection in these verses between pastoral leadership and preaching. When Paul warns the young pastor to "have nothing to do with irreverent, silly myths" (1 Tim. 4:7), he does it right on the heels of noting "the words of the faith and of the good doctrine" that Timothy has followed and is responsible for teaching to his congregation (1 Tim. 4:6). Like Christians today, believers in Timothy's church were being assaulted with perversions of God's truth. Old Testament history was being contaminated with concocted legends, and genealogies were being stripped of their literal value and interpreted symbolically. All of this was syncretized with demonic asceticism that promised spiritual elitism through sexual abstinence and dietary restrictions.[4]

So, Paul compels Timothy to contend for the faith by countering such heresy with the proclamation of sound doctrine. Like Jude, the apostle probably would have preferred to write to his mentee and talk about the grandeur of the believer's salvation. But the onslaught of false doctrine was making it necessary to convince the young pastor "to contend for the faith that was once for all delivered to the saints" (Jude 3). Such is the charge of every pastor. God's truth is the only real counter to the enemy's lies. The practice of explaining that nourishing truth stands in

4   R. Kent Hughes and Bryan Chapell, *1 and 2 Timothy and Titus: To Guard the Deposit*, Preaching the Word (Wheaton, IL: Crossway, 2000), 106–7.

stark contrast to feeding people the empty calories of fables, myths, old wives' tales, and the wisdom of the world, all of which are completely devoid of God and, therefore, contain no power to foster godlikeness in anyone's life (Col. 2:22–23).

God has ordained his truth to be the primary agent of growing believers in godliness (1 Pet. 2:2). Jesus prayed to his Father, "Sanctify them in the truth; your word is truth" (John 17:17). As pastors, we can lead our people to a lot of things. Godliness must be at the top of the list, both for ourselves and our congregations. In all our leading, scriptural leadership requires us to lead them to this destination through the faithful exposition of God's truth, the only thing that can transform them into his image.

### The Pastor's Communication Is Compelling

Like many seminaries, our school's preaching curriculum contains a practical exercise where students preach to the class and then receive feedback from their peers and professor. Semester after semester, the same struggles surface for many young preachers. One of the most frequent weaknesses is the failure to preach with authority. "Convince me that what you're saying is important," we find ourselves repeating. "Preach like you believe what you're saying!"

The failure to speak authoritatively in preaching probably comes from several places. One is simply the nervousness that naturally results from inexperience (not to mention preaching in front of your peers and your professor!). Another influence is the fear of coming across as authoritarian or arrogant. A third stimulus is probably the trend in contemporary preaching toward being more conversational and less confrontational. Regardless of where it originates, passive preaching that is less than compelling and lacks authority is all too common in the contemporary church.

The apostle Paul would have none of that from his youthful disciple. "Command and teach these things," he instructed Timothy (1 Tim. 4:11). These words highlight the preaching ministry as the theme of the rest of this paragraph. As a basis for expositional leadership, they also serve as an obvious intersection between Timothy's leadership, preaching, and pastoral ministry. The word "command" means to prescribe, to order, or to mandate with authority. The word "teach" carries the idea of instructing people. Together, they're Paul's way of directing Timothy to educate his congregants in the truth and exhort them to obey it. Overall, this combination is frequent in the pastoral epistles (e.g., 1 Tim. 6:2; 2 Tim. 2:2; Titus 2:15). Paul wants Timothy to preach in such a way that his listeners sense the weightiness of his words and at the same time feel equipped to obey them. Paul wanted him to communicate God's truth in a compelling way.

Following the charge to command and compel his people probably didn't come easy for this young pastor. Like pastors in today's church, Timothy had a lot working against him. He was facing cultural pressure as Rome began to crumble and Emperor Nero turned up the heat on Christ followers. In fact, Timothy was about to lose his mentor, the voice of the Christian movement, who had a target on his back and was facing inevitable execution at the hands of the Roman government. Timothy was inexperienced, so some of the people in his church had a problem following his leadership (1 Tim. 4:12). He also was a little sickly at times, leading Paul to prescribe medicine for him (1 Tim. 5:23). On top of all these things, a survey of Paul's epistles shows that Timothy was a naturally timid person (e.g., 2 Tim. 1:7–8; 1 Cor. 16:10–11). Skills like working a room and taking charge didn't come easily for him. All these things surely played a role in tempting Timothy to be a little reserved in his preaching.

Most of us pastors can identify with at least a few of the things Timothy was facing. We feel the pushback against our ministry and message from our increasingly secular culture. We know the sense of loneliness and anxiety that comes when mentors are no longer around. We can be intimidated by our lack of experience in ministry leadership or unfamiliarity with a new ministry assignment. Some of us navigate debilitating health problems, either in our own lives or the lives of family members. And many pastors know what it means to be naturally timid or lacking in gifts that seem most conducive for public speaking and other aspects of pastoral leadership. All these realities and more can undermine a pastor's confidence when he rises to preach, causing him to throttle back a bit in his communication and speak with less authority.

So, what is a pastor to do when he is reserved in his public proclamation for personal or circumstantial reasons? The object in Paul's instructions holds the key: "Command and teach these things" (1 Tim. 4:11). We noted earlier that the apostle frequently uses the phrase "these things" in this letter to encapsulate the practical and doctrinal issues that he's calling Timothy to address in his pastoral leadership. However, it's important that, on this side of a closed canon, we understand "these things" to represent more than instructions limited to the cultural and doctrinal subjects he addressed.

Paul's use of "these things" represents for us the whole of apostolic teaching and even the totality of biblical revelation. The apostle Peter will later even verify that Paul's writings are to be viewed on the same level as the rest of inspired Scripture (2 Pet. 3:15–16). And in his next letter to Timothy, Paul will say, "What you have heard from me in the presence of many witnesses entrust to faithful men, who will be able to teach others also" (2 Tim. 2:2). Everything God commanded Timothy to be and do through the proclamation and pen of the apostle Paul was to be commanded to Timothy's audience who would then command others. And so, this stewardship has continued throughout Christian history, even until now.

This is where the pastor's authority lies. This is why we can command and compel in our preaching. Today, we preach under the authority of apostolic instruction, and our content comes from the record of God's supernatural revelation that we know to be inerrant, infallible, and sufficient to accomplish God's redemptive purposes in people's lives. Our message is not our own. Overall, the Bible uses several different images to describe the derived authority that characterizes preaching. We're called stewards because we are entrusted with someone else's possession. We're called sowers because we scatter someone else's seed.

We're called heralds because we carry someone else's message. We're called ambassadors because we represent someone else! We preach under an authority that isn't our own, and we communicate a message that didn't originate with us.

Not only do we stand in a long heritage of apostolic authority but we also stand in a long line of faithful expositors. Our delegated authority and entrusted message mean that we must accurately represent the one who commissioned us. What we say must rightly reflect the nature and the message of the Lord we represent. Exposition is not a sermon form, it's a process. It's the process of interpreting "these things" that God has spoken and then explaining them to contemporary listeners so they can hear his voice and be transformed into his image.

### The Pastor's Esteem Is Earned

"Preach the Gospel at all times, and if necessary use words." This familiar saying is most frequently credited to Francis of Assisi, but its true origin is unknown. Whoever said it obviously felt like the most important aspect of our gospel witness is the way we live our lives. But in reality, that assertion is quite misleading. You can live a moral life with impeccable integrity and yet people can still die and go to hell wondering what made the difference in your life. Unless people hear the gospel message and embrace it, they can't be saved (Rom. 10:14; Col. 4:5–6; 1 Pet. 3:15).

The shortsightedness of this saying, however, does not negate the reality that there is a relationship between what we say and how we act. This is certainly true in pastoral preaching. The apostle Paul knows that young Timothy, probably in his early- to mid-thirties at the time, is experiencing some pushback against his pastoral leadership. Some of the people don't esteem him very highly because of his age. Such a response is understandable when a young guy is standing up in front of a crowd commanding and teaching (1 Tim. 4:11) people who are older than him. So Paul encourages him, "Let no one despise you for your youth" (1 Tim. 4:12). When Timothy stands up to preach, Paul doesn't want his people to look down on him and dismiss his teaching simply because he's young.

Some things are objective in the world. A person's age and level of experience are among them. So what is Timothy supposed to do? He can't walk into the room one day and announce to his congregation that he's now identifying as a fifty-year-old. And, certainly, it isn't an acceptable option for him to stop preaching. The aged apostle has an answer. "Set the believers an example," Paul tells the youthful preacher, "in speech, in conduct, in love, in faith, in purity" (1 Tim. 4:12). Instead of Timothy's preaching being undermined by his age, Paul says, it can be enhanced by his example. In other words, he can earn the people's esteem by his actions.

It is here that we see the intersection between leadership, preaching, and pastoral ministry. A pastor can dispel a lot of criticism about his leadership (including his preaching) by supporting his authority in the pulpit with a life well lived outside the pulpit. This includes the whole spectrum of life. According to Paul, it means our "speech" should be wholesome, edifying, honest, tasteful, guarded, wise, and humble. It means that when we are at the ballpark or grocery store our "conduct" should be righteous and above reproach. It means our entire lives should be lived "in love, in faith, in purity," just like the life of Jesus who lives within us.

The congruence between our online leadership in the pulpit and our offline leadership as a godly example also guards against us abusing our authority over the people we shepherd. Peter says that pastors are "not [to be] domineering over those in [their] charge, but . . . examples to the flock" (1 Pet. 5:3). Paul instructs Timothy to lead and instruct his church members as family (1 Tim. 4:6; 5:1–2). We don't boss family around, belittle them like they're no-good losers, or bully them into acting properly (as is often associated with some pastoral preaching). Rather, Paul says we're to set an example for our people by the way we live, which implies a desire for them to emulate us (1 Cor. 11:1). We want our church members to honor Christ in their lives, so we give them examples to follow like parents do for their children. If we approach pastoral ministry with this perspective, we'll be able to give strong leadership to our people both inside and outside the pulpit.

Whether your inexperience is due to your age or having a fresh start in a new ministry field, people won't be able to look down on you if they have to look up to your actions. They won't reject you for your inexperience if they respect you for your integrity; they won't hate on you for your inexperience if they hold you up in high esteem. On the other hand, we can't expect people to respect us simply because we hold the office of pastor or engage in the ministry of preaching. Thus, as part of our scriptural leadership, we must earn their esteem by the way we live and lead in every area of life and ministry.

### The Pastor's Priority Is Preaching

While preaching isn't the only way a pastor leads, it ought to be the first way he leads, at least as far as his public ministry goes. Preaching is just about the only ministry in which a pastor engages every single week (sometimes multiple times) and just about the only ministry he exercises when all his people are expected to be present. It's the time when he gets to speak to the greatest number of people, and it comes around regularly like clockwork. The pastor of a local church does a lot of things—personal evangelism and disciple making, vision and strategy development, meetings, counseling, visitation, weddings, funerals, and more—but his top priority is the ministry through which he addresses the greatest number of people on the most frequent basis.

The apostle Paul wants Timothy to have his priorities right. So, he tells him to "devote [himself] to the public reading of Scripture, to exhortation, to teaching" (1 Tim. 4:13). About this directive, R. Kent Hughes and Bryan Chapell assert, "This simple sentence is a landmark text in defining the major work of the pastor and the worship of the church."[5] The verb "devote" means to give oneself to something. This

---

5   Hughes and Chapell, *1 and 2 Timothy and Titus*, 115.

work is to be Timothy's priority. Furthermore, the word "implies previous preparation in private."[6] Timothy is not just to give himself to the public work, but to the study and preparation it takes to get ready to do it—"it [is] to be his way of life."[7]

According to Paul, this primary work to which Timothy, and every pastor, is called to devote his life includes three essential aspects—reading, exhortation, and teaching. First, "the public reading of Scripture" involves reading it aloud in the public worship service. Second, "exhortation," sometimes translated as "preaching," is pressing the truth of the passage on the people's consciences by way of challenge, rebuke, persuasion, plea, counsel, and comfort. This is equivalent to application but not limited to practical ways to act on the truth. It involves sincerely appealing to people's wills to obey, identifying the blessings when they do, and warning them of the consequences when they don't. Third, "teaching" is explaining the meaning of the text. While exhortation appeals to the will, teaching appeals to the intellect and provides the necessary information for hearers to understand the truth and respond rightly.

Needless to say, that's a pretty good description of biblical exposition! Paul says the young pastor is to read Scripture aloud, help people understand it, and compel them to obey it. To say it another way: read it, explain it, apply it. In some respect, these three elements are the irreducible minimums and nonnegotiables that qualify preaching as expository. John Stott says,

> It was already customary in the synagogue for the reading of Scripture to be followed by an exposition, and this practice was carried over into the Christian assemblies, being the origin of the sermon in public worship. It was taken for granted from the beginning that Christian preaching would be expository preaching, that is, that all

6   Donald Guthrie, *Pastoral Epistles: An Introduction and Commentary*, vol. 14 of *Tyndale New Testament Commentaries* (Downers Grove, IL: InterVarsity Press, 1990), 111.

7   John F. MacArthur, *1 Timothy*, MacArthur New Testament Commentary (Chicago: Moody, 1995), 175–76.

Christian instruction and exhortation would be drawn out of the passage which had been read.[8]

We call this work "exposition" because it involves the process of peeling back the layers of time, culture, language, context, and other elements that characterize biblical revelation for the purpose of *exposing* God's voice to people.

The union between pastoral leadership and biblical exposition is clear. Preaching is obviously not the only way a pastor leads, but it is arguably the most important. While a pastor provides leadership in all the ministries mentioned earlier, none are more effectual than the regular times he opens the Scriptures and leads God's people to hear his voice, understand what he's saying, and say yes to it. We've already seen the importance of the pastor leading by example, something that can make or break his effectiveness as a preacher. But the pastor's example, like other mediums of leadership, gets limited airtime in comparison to his work as a preacher. Preaching provides the best venue for leading and exercising influence on the flock that's been entrusted to his care. Thus, scriptural leadership requires preaching to be our priority.

## The Pastor's Calling Is Critical

Ordination is somewhat of a convoluted concept in today's church. Most Christians see it as the process of setting an individual apart from the laity as clergy and authorizing them to perform various religious duties. Some denominations require it, but others don't. Some ministers have been formally ordained, while others haven't. Some people believe it's a biblical concept, and others believe Scripture is silent on the subject. Tragically, even many denominations, churches, and individuals who do embrace it do so as a mere formality. Often it's approached as a mere rubber stamp for being able to perform wedding ceremonies or opting out of social security with the IRS.

8   Stott, *Guard the Truth*, 121–22.

Regardless of what we call it, or even whether we embrace it as a formal practice, the apostle Paul implied that the local church is to engage in some method of setting individuals apart for Christian leadership. He told Timothy, "Do not neglect the gift you have, which was given you by prophecy when the council of elders laid their hands on you" (1 Tim. 4:14). He would later appeal to it again, saying, "I remind you to fan into flame the gift of God, which is in you through the laying on of my hands" (2 Tim. 1:6). Obviously, for Paul, this process wasn't merely a formality, licensure, or tax benefit. Whatever it entails, it appears to play a weighty (even supernatural!) role in the call of God on Timothy's life. And Timothy must be faithful to it.

What is Paul talking about? While we don't have all the historical information we would like to have about this process, it appears that three parts—gift, prophecy, and laying on of hands—comprised Timothy's calling from God. "Prophecy" was how the Holy Spirit called him (1 Tim. 1:18), in much the same way the Spirit "called" Paul and Barnabas in Antioch (Acts 13:1–3). The "council of elders" laying their hands on him was the church's recognition, acknowledgment, and confirmation of that calling. Both elements underscore the crucial and spiritual role local churches play in the calling of men to gospel ministry. Sometimes an individual senses God's call first and then the church confirms it. Other times the church recognizes the call first and then encourages the individual to respond to it. Overall, God's call to gospel ministry rarely comes in isolation—most often it occurs as a beautiful partnership between Christ's Spirit and his body.

But what exactly is this "gift" that Timothy has been given? Opinions regarding its exact nature are all over the map. It's been identified as the spiritual ability to build up the church, rule the church, and discern between what's true and what's false.[9] But the common denominator in many perspectives is that it had something to do with Timothy's preaching,[10] a ministry that certainly encompassed all these other

9   Stott, *Guard the Truth*, 122.
10  See Fee, *1 and 2 Timothy, Titus*, 108; Thomas D. Lea and Hayne P. Griffin, *1, 2 Timothy, Titus* (Nashville: B&H, 1992), 139; Stott, *Guard the Truth*, 122; Hughes and Chapell, *1 and 2 Timothy and Titus*, 117; MacArthur, *1 Timothy*, 179.

leadership tasks. This conclusion is supported by the immediate context of our passage, 1 Timothy 4:6–16, as well as the frequent exhortations Paul gives Timothy in his second letter to minister God's word faithfully (2 Tim. 2:15, 24–26; 3:14–4:5).

The core of Paul's exhortation, however, isn't just a repeated appeal for Timothy to exercise his gift of preaching. The imperative "Do not neglect" in the language of the New Testament suggests that Timothy probably has been showing some signs of avoiding (if not abandoning) his call to preach and that he should stop doing so immediately. Later Paul will tell him to "fan into flame [this] gift of God" (2 Tim. 1:6), implying that his endowment is not automatic or even permanent if left unattended. Hughes and Chapell identify this call and giftedness to preach as a "use it or lose it" enterprise.[11] If the man of God abandons or even neglects his preaching gift for ungodly reasons, he stands in danger of losing it and becoming a statistic in the large number of men who leave the ministry every year. The stakes are high and the time is short. Pastors must rise to the occasion and steward their ministry callings. This call is critical in gospel advancement and the church's fulfillment of Christ's mission.

Once again, like the instructions about reading, exhorting, and teaching in the previous verse, the connection between pastoral leadership and preaching in the current exhortation is inherent. Pastors have been given the supernatural "gift" to lead the church, and our leadership is inextricably tied to our calling to preach. Therefore, we must embrace and nurture that calling. We lead in a variety of ways—edifying the church, overseeing the church, discerning between true and false doctrine, and much more. But all these areas of leadership are either carried out or supported by our ministry in the pulpit. We are called to faithfully expound God's word so that individual believers are shaped into Christ's image and our congregations follow us as undershepherds while we lead them to corporate Christlikeness.

---

11   Hughes and Chapell, *1 and 2 Timothy and Titus*, 117.

## The Pastor's Life Is Leveraged

"God first. Family second. Church third." This set of priorities—and its order—has been declared by a lot of pastoral candidates to a lot of search committees. The combination and sequence sounds very spiritual, especially when it is expressed as a pastor's desire to not let the busyness of church ministry adversely affect his family. But is it biblical? Does a man's family rank higher on a pastor's priority list than the body of Christ? The gospel? The Great Commission? Jesus said, "If anyone comes to me and does not hate his father and mother and wife and children and brothers and sisters, yes, and even his own life, he cannot be my disciple" (Luke 14:26; Matt. 10:37). It sounds like our Lord might not have that same list of priorities.

To be sure, Jesus does not want the pastor's ministry to cause him to lose or neglect his family. But neither does he want the pastor's family or anything else to keep him from spending himself on his ministry calling. Paul compels Timothy to "practice these things, immerse yourself in them" (1 Tim. 4:15). The term "practice" carries the idea of thinking about, meditating on, or planning for. The word "immerse" literally means to "be in." Together, these two imperatives suggest that a preacher of the gospel is to be absorbed with his preaching ministry in both thought and action, both preparation and practice. Doing so does not necessitate neglecting his family. While it may require wisdom and balance, Jesus never calls us to anything for which his grace isn't sufficient. And two things can both be true at the same time without compromising either. The pastor can be a faithful husband and father while simultaneously obeying his call to leverage his life for the proclamation of the gospel.

The core components of leadership, preaching, and pastoral ministry are woven into Paul's reason for encouraging Timothy to spend himself on his preaching "so that all may see [his] progress" (1 Tim. 4:15). Later Paul will use the verbal form of the word "progress" to describe people regressing in ungodliness (2 Tim. 2:16; 3:9). But here he's using the term to describe Timothy's "development in the teachings of godliness that accord with the gospel."[12] Stott describes this dynamic well:

> People should be able to observe not only what [Christian leaders] are but what they are becoming, supplying evidence that they are growing into maturity in Christ. Some Christian leaders imagine that they have to appear perfect, with no visible flaws or blemishes. But there are at least two reasons why this is a mistake. First, it is hypocritical. Since none of us is a paragon of all virtues, it is dishonest to pretend to be. Secondly, the pretense [sic] discourages people, who then suppose that their leaders are altogether exceptional and even inhuman.[13]

At no time in our ministries as pastors do people observe our growth in godliness more than as they listen to us preach week by week. They see and hear our authenticity, humanity, and progress. They see and hear us continue to grow and learn. They see and hear us leverage everything to preach the word. As a result, they are encouraged, inspired, and equipped to follow our lead to the destination of looking more like Jesus. After all, Jesus leveraged his entire life so that could be a reality.

## The Pastor's Integrity Is Indispensable

It's been refreshing to see a heightened emphasis on integrity in recent years. There seems to be a kind of revival of it in many sectors of life, including politics, entertainment, and business. According to Jeff Iorg, "a person of integrity is a whole, complete, undivided person—not segmented or fractionalized. No double-dealing, no double standards, and no double meanings! A person is whole, complete, undivided in words and actions and standards."[14] To have integrity implies a consistency between what's on the inside of a person and what's on the outside.

---

12   Lea and Griffin, *1, 2 Timothy, Titus*, 140.
13   Stott, *Guard the Truth*, 123–24.
14   Jeff Iorg, *The Character of Leadership* (Nashville: B&H, 2007), 24.

In no sector of life is integrity more indispensable than in gospel ministry. For ten verses now the great apostle has been shepherding his young protégé in the relationship between his leadership, pastoral responsibilities, and public preaching ministry. Now, in somewhat of a summary statement of everything that has preceded it, the intersection between these dimensions once again is low-hanging fruit. In this exhortation, Paul speaks directly about leadership both in and out of the pulpit: "Keep a close watch on yourself and on the teaching" (1 Tim. 4:16). This imperative compels Timothy to give careful attention ("keep a close watch") to his character and conduct ("on yourself") as well as the doctrine that he teaches ("on the teaching").

While Paul certainly wants integrity to be characteristic of both pastoral leadership and preaching as individual dimensions of the pastor's ministry, he seems more concerned here that they demonstrate integrity in both of these at the same time. In other words, he charges us to make sure there's consistency between our personal lives and our preaching ministries. Our absorption with preaching (1 Tim. 4:15) can't be allowed to make us abandon the care of our souls. Likewise, our personal soul care can never be allowed to make us neglect our preaching ministry to our congregations. There must be a consistency between the time and attention we give to these components because collectively they will determine our effectiveness as pastors.

Integrity between our public ministry and our private lives is vital because, according to Paul, the stakes are high. He says to "persist in this, for by so doing you will save both yourself and your hearers" (1 Tim. 4:16). Our endurance in maintaining such a balance is essential for eternal salvation, both for ourselves as well as our people. Our persistence doesn't earn this salvation, but it does give public testimony to its reality. Thomas D. Lea and Hayne P. Griffin explain,

> It is not that Timothy's endurance would merit salvation but that a stamina that produced holiness and doctrinal orthodoxy gave incontrovertible evidence of heading for salvation. Second, Paul suggested that the obedient perseverance of the preacher is an important factor

in the endurance of the hearers. The preacher's model of persever-
ance builds the same trait in his flock. The stumbles and fumbles of
a wandering spiritual leader will infect a congregation with a variety
of spiritual sicknesses.[15]

The combination and consistency between godliness in our lives
and godliness expounded from our pulpits is both an agent and evidence of salvation. God graciously uses this potent gospel formula to
compel our listeners to respond to the faithful exposition of his word.
This is why our integrity is indispensable for scriptural leadership.

## Conclusion

In our contemporary Christian culture, pastors are constantly bom-
barded with leadership materials and messages, many of which are
hard to distinguish from secular business philosophies. Sadly, many
ministry leaders have embraced these worldly principles and combined
them with trendy approaches in their efforts to stay relevant in a very
fluid culture. Even though these pastors are often celebrated, their
leadership is typically compromised by diluted messages that fail to
honor the biblical text because it doesn't serve their attempts at social
influence and cultural relevance.

Ironically, expository preaching is hailed as the antidote, but it too
suffers from similar inconsistencies. Oftentimes its proponents define
it broadly and endorse it ceremoniously without a clear understanding of its nature or practice. Sadly, this can result in people dismissing
Scripture as irrelevant and disregarding preaching as religious rants.
When the distorted solution only serves to compound leadership issues in the modern church, God's people find themselves "harassed
and helpless, like sheep without a shepherd" (Matt. 9:36).

Against these various and influential "winds of doctrine," what is
the secret of shepherding God's people well? The beginning point,
at least, is being gripped by a theology of preaching and pastoral

15  Lea and Griffin, *1, 2 Timothy, Titus*, 141.

leadership that flows from the pages of God's holy word. Stott argues for this essential ordering, challenging pastors to allow their doctrinal commitments to determine their practical approach: "The essential secret is not mastering certain techniques but being mastered by certain convictions."[16] This insightful exhortation about maintaining our motivation to preach in a world that doesn't want to listen reminds us that our theology must determine our methodology.

Overall, this crucial order must be maintained for leading through exposition, two tasks that many pastors don't even see as belonging in the same sentence but that actually are wedded together by the biblical truths that undergird them both. And while Paul's words in 1 Timothy 4 don't serve as an exhaustive biblical foundation for such a work, they do provide a solid starting place for seeing how God intends biblical exposition and pastoral leadership to work in tandem as scriptural leadership.

16  Stott, *Between Two Worlds*, 92.

# 2

# Spiritual Leadership from the Pulpit

*My speech and my message were not in plausible words of*
*wisdom, but in demonstration of the Spirit and of power.*

1 CORINTHIANS 2:4

HAVE YOU EVER NOTICED how a brand name can become synonymous with the generic name for an object? Perhaps you've offered
someone a Kleenex without actually considering what type of facial
tissue you're really sharing (e.g., Puffs, Scotts, or an actual Kleenex!).
Maybe you've sat down in your La-Z-Boy without the intention of
referencing the actual brand of your recliner or referred to a random
electronic tablet as an iPad. When it comes to household items like
tissues, furniture, and personal devices, as long as you know what
you're referring to, what you call it really doesn't matter. But when
you're discussing something significant, being precise and specific
is crucial.

Oftentimes when we refer to things as "spiritual" we're simply using
a generic term to reference something related to our Christian faith.
We also use it to distinguish a subject from its secular counterpart,
like spiritual leadership as compared with secular leadership. But as
we consider how God intends for us to leverage the pulpit to shepherd
his people, we must understand "spiritual" as a more intentional and

deliberate term that references the person and work of the Holy Spirit in expositional leadership.

In order to effectively exert spiritual leadership through our preaching, we must consider how biblical exposition facilitates the work of God's Spirit in our lives and in the lives of his people. This involves identifying ways that we may be inadvertently stifling or disregarding his work as well as exploring ways we can more intentionally submit to him as an extension of his leadership. Overall, there are three facets of our preaching ministry directly related to pastoral leadership that must be decisively spiritual—our sermon preparation, sermon delivery, and sermon application.

## Spirit-Encountered Sermon Preparation

For most of us, sermon preparation follows a weekly rhythm and involves an established routine. Whether you set aside your mornings, a particular day of the week, or designate some other blocks in your schedule, it's important to allocate enough time in the study to faithfully prepare your messages. Within these personalized time frames each of us also has our own approach to sermon development. Our time studying the text, reading commentaries, constructing an outline, organizing the message, and making final tweaks is typically based on our personal preferences and schedules.

Over time, as we refine our process, it becomes efficient and serves us well. But if we're not careful, our routine can become redundant, our study can become sterile, and our preaching may then become powerless. In order to preserve the vibrancy and intimacy of our sermon preparation and avoid these habit hazards, it is crucial for us to recognize how we can encounter the Spirit and engage in his work through our sermon preparation process.

Encountering the Spirit in our preparation centers on the inherent relationship between the Spirit and the text. The Scriptures are the written expression of God's divine revelation. In essence, he "breathed" them out through the biblical writers (2 Tim. 3:16). More specifically, the human authors of Scripture "spoke from God as they were carried along by the Spirit" (2 Pet. 1:21). The Spirit's role in the supernatural work of inspiration undergirds his essential role in interpretation as well. Jesus described the Spirit's interpretive role as the one who would "teach you all things" and "guide you into all the truth" (John 14:26; 16:13). Likewise, Paul explained that apart from the Spirit, we're unable to discern God's thoughts and his truth. But the Spirit freely discloses them to us so that by "interpreting spiritual truths" we can share them with "those who are spiritual" (1 Cor. 2:10–13).

As we study the text of Scripture and prepare our sermons, we must not simply rely on a method or formulaic approach that ignores our dependence on the Spirit. Rather, we must yield to his interpretive guidance, which begins with demonstrating our dependence on him through prayer. Our humble petitions before the Lord should expose our hearts to him as we confess and repent of sin so that we might be "set apart as holy, useful to the master" (2 Tim. 2:21). In addition, our pleas should acknowledge our inability to properly understand and interpret a passage apart from his enabling presence. This doesn't mean that we're looking to create some mystical experience; it simply acknowledges that any understanding of the Scriptures that we have has graciously been revealed to us. This takes the pressure off of us to come up with some clever or unique interpretation of a passage. It also provides us with confidence that the Spirit who inspired the text will disclose its meaning to us as we submit ourselves to him in prayerful humility and careful study.

Perhaps even more importantly, our encounter with the Spirit through the text goes beyond his inspiration and interpretive role. When we read the Scriptures, we are personally engaging with the Lord himself—we hear him speak. Thus, the Bible regularly references the Scriptures with the voice of the Spirit. For example, in Acts, David's written words are equated with what "the Holy Spirit spoke" (Acts 1:16; 4:25). Likewise, as the apostle John declares the word of the Lord, he repeatedly calls us to "hear what the Spirit says to the churches" (Rev. 2:7, 11, 17, 29; 3:6, 13, 22). In other words, when we come to the text of Scripture, we are encountering the presence of God's Spirit and listening to his voice.

Practically speaking, we can understand it like this: the Spirit continues to speak through what he has spoken. This is why we understand the Scriptures as "living and active," powerful and effective, and able to accomplish God's purpose in the lives of his people (Heb. 4:12; cf. Isa. 55:10–11). The Bible is the voice of the eternal Spirit (Heb. 9:14) who communicates timeless truth that is perpetually relevant for all generations and abides forever (1 Pet. 1:25). Therefore, when we immerse ourselves in God's word, we are not simply studying to prepare a message; we are entering into his presence and encountering his Spirit.

This has two major implications for us as preachers. First, as we encounter the Spirit through the word, we must seek to be transformed. We often stress the importance of applying the truth of the text to our lives as pastors before preaching the passage, and rightfully so. But it goes beyond simply implementing points of textual application into our lives—we must be changed as a result of being in the presence of God. When Moses came down from Mount Sinai speaking with God (Ex. 34:29–35) and the apostles stood before their accusers at the Sanhedrin (Acts 4:13), it was evident that they had been with the Lord. The same must be true of us—our lives must be different as a result of encountering God's Spirit through his word. This should change how we approach the text and our sermon preparation. Abiding fellowship with the Lord and the resulting life transformation should be our primary and ultimate goal!

The second implication of encountering the Spirit through his word relates to our sermons and our people. Similar to how this fact changes our approach to studying the Scriptures, it also alters our approach to expounding them and our people's approach to listening to them. We will help our people recognize the supernatural power of God's word and teach them to approach it as a divine encounter by revering the text when we open the Scriptures. This involves both carefully explaining God's word and confidently declaring, "Thus says the Lord." Our sermons must be so clearly text driven that our people learn to relish their encounter with the Lord through the Scriptures and don't mistake our voice for the Spirit's. That, at its most foundational level, is spiritual leadership through exposition.

In addition to the symbiotic relationship between the Spirit and the text, Spirit-encountered preparation also requires us to consider the Spirit of the text—the divine interpreter and his intended implications of the passage. To be clear, this is not meant to imply that there is a mystical meaning to be discovered. We affirm and practice the historical, grammatical, theological exegesis that locates meaning in the author's original intent. In addition, we also acknowledge that the divine author's intention, which never conflicts with the biblical writer, transcends the immediate context and expands meaning across redemptive history through the progressive revelation of the word, both living and written. Therefore, the meaning of a passage, grounded in the author's intent as expressed in the text, has significance and application for all people throughout history, including our listeners! For preachers, this fact is crucial because it verifies the timeless relevance of all Scripture as we proclaim the historical text to a contemporary audience.

Yet, we must also recognize "the spirit of the text," which means acknowledging that a literal understanding of Scripture does not rigidly restrict the interpretation of a verse or passage in a way that negates the spiritual implications inherent within a specific command or principle. The text doesn't mean less than the explicitly stated truth, but the immeasurable depths of God's word includes so much more for us to explore and expound. Perhaps the most obvious example is Jesus's clarification of Old Testament statutes in the Sermon on the Mount. By using six specific citations, he explains the idea that the intended "letter of the law" always included "the spirit of the law" (Matt. 5:21–48). While this does not give us license to go beyond what a text says and pronounce our ideas as binding and authoritative, it does challenge us to go beneath the surface of the text to understand the biblical and theological underpinnings of the passage that promote genuine obedience rather than superficial compliance.

In order to plumb these depths, we must encounter the spirit of the text by recognizing that the eternal significance of the Bible is not simply the result of enduring truths and principles but derives from the Scriptures' ultimate source and fulfillment, which is rooted in Christ. Jesus affirmed this reality by declaring that he came to fulfill the Law and the Prophets (Matt. 5:17). He also demonstrated this hermeneutic to his disciples: "beginning with Moses and all the Prophets, he interpreted to them in all the Scriptures the things concerning himself" (Luke 24:27). And he further clarified for his followers by saying "everything written about [him] in the Law of Moses and the Prophets and the Psalms" is fulfilled in his redemptive work and resurrection (Luke 24:44).

This Christ-centered view of Scripture and its subsequent hermeneutic reflects the Spirit's primary role of glorifying Christ and testifying to him (John 16:14–15). In other words, the Scriptures were always intended to find their ultimate meaning and fulfillment in Jesus as a result of the Spirit's work as the divine agent of inspiration. Therefore, as the Spirit guides our interpretation, we must discern the Christ-centered meaning of the passage that reveals an aspect of our sinful condition, the redemptive truth in the text that is ultimately accomplished in Christ, and the faith response that transforms us into the likeness of Jesus. And this transforming work is also accomplished by the Spirit (2 Cor. 3:18)!

As we encounter the Spirit of the text in our preparation, he helps us interpret a passage and develop a sermon that honors his intended meaning of the text by exalting Christ. In addition, the Spirit works to conform us to the likeness of Jesus so that we might entreat our hearers to be transformed by the power of the gospel through the truth of God's word. When we magnify Christ in our lives and in our sermons through Spirit-encountered preparation, we cooperate with the work of the Spirit and lead our people to encounter his presence and life changing power for themselves. This epitomizes spiritual leadership from the pulpit.

### Spirit-Empowered Sermon Delivery

Perhaps the most common aspect of preaching that's associated with the work of the Spirit is our sermon delivery. Since Scripture doesn't include a list of characteristics that constitute Spirit-filled preaching, it's difficult to establish definitive criteria and attribute a preacher's delivery to the Spirit. Many people associate animated enthusiasm and vigorous zeal with anointed preaching, but these qualities aren't necessarily synonymous with the Spirit's work in Scripture. Although the concept of divine empowerment for preaching is clearly referenced in the Bible (Acts 4:31; Luke 4:18; 1 Cor. 2:4), it's not explicitly defined. Based on its biblical description, Greg Heisler argues that "Spirit-empowerment" is a more helpful term because it avoids the stereotyped understanding of "anointing" and captures "the dynamic of the Spirit's power for preaching."[1]

While there may be some confusion regarding the more conventional descriptions of Spirit-filled preaching, our sermon delivery will undoubtedly be an essential part of our spiritual leadership from the pulpit. Thus, it's important for us to consider what Spirit-empowered delivery involves. There aren't specific delivery characteristics we can designate and develop, and we can't manufacture the Spirit's presence. Instead, his divine empowerment begins in prayer.

Overall, the Spirit is essential to every aspect of our prayer life since we're encouraged to bow before the Lord, "praying at all times *in the Spirit* with all prayer and supplication" (Eph. 6:18). But interestingly, Paul's appeal to the Ephesians to pray in the Spirit on his behalf included his request that "words may be given to me in opening my mouth boldly to proclaim the mystery of the gospel . . . that I may declare it boldly, as I ought to speak" (Eph. 6:19–20). Likewise, he appealed to the Colossians, "At the same time, pray also for us, that God may open to us a door for the word, to declare the mystery of Christ . . . that I may make it clear, which is how I ought to speak" (Col. 4:3–4). It's clear from Paul's prayers and his intercessory requests that various aspects of

---

1    Greg Heisler, *Spirit-Led Preaching: The Holy Spirit's Role in Sermon Preparation and Delivery*, rev. ed. (Nashville: B&H, 2018), 161. Heisler's book provides a thorough consideration of the role of the Spirit in preaching. Chapter 10 is dedicated to the subject of the Holy Spirit and anointing and examines the concept from a biblical and homiletical perspective, including helps and hindrances to the Spirit's empowerment in preaching.

his Spirit-empowered delivery, from his boldness to his clarity, would begin with Spirit-led prayer.

As we pray for God's divine empowerment, there are some crucial aspects of sermon delivery that cooperate with the work of the Spirit and can facilitate his power in our preaching. One definitive quality of Spirit-empowered proclamation that should characterize our sermon delivery is inspired passion. This attribute is not to be equated with emotional fervency, vocal intensity, or verbal ingenuity. In fact, Paul characterized his preaching as quite the opposite. He described it with terms like "weakness," "fear and much trembling," and without "plausible words of wisdom" (1 Cor. 2:3–4). At the same time, he asserted that his preaching was "in demonstration of the Spirit and of power" (1 Cor. 2:3). So, if it wasn't exuberance, eloquence, or oratory skill, what qualified his preaching as a manifestation of the Spirit and power? It was Paul's overwhelming conviction that when he preached, he was "proclaiming . . . the testimony of God," namely, "Jesus Christ and him crucified" (1 Cor. 2:1–2; cf. 2 Cor. 4:5).

In other words, preaching with inspired passion is defined by a conviction that derives from the divine nature of Scripture and the life changing power of the gospel. These realities empower us to preach with a deep-seated certainty in God's word and humble reliance on the Spirit. This translates into assurance and boldness in the pulpit, but not arrogance and brashness. Rather, our delivery should communicate an unwavering trust in the authority, reliability, and sufficiency of Scripture. Simply put, when we put our confidence in the Spirit-inspired Scripture, it results in Spirit-empowered preaching.

The nature of God's word is also the basis for another aspect of our inspired passion—the tone and expression of the text. Our affirmation of verbal plenary inspiration rightly emphasizes the details of the text, from the terms to their tenses. But our sermon design and delivery should consider the tone of the text as well because the emotional sense and disposition of the passage is also inspired by the Spirit and communicates aspects of meaning, significance, and the intended response of the reader. In other words, the tone of the text should shape the disposition of our sermon delivery.[2]

This means that our passionate delivery should not be primarily determined by our natural disposition, our personal feelings, or the age and enthusiasm of our listeners. While all of these can be influential factors to consider for effective communication, the prevailing factor for our sermon delivery must be the sense and tone of the text. From a literary perspective, these aspects of the text are often distinguished by genre. For example, prophetic texts often carry a sense of emphatic declaration that is expressed with gravity and urgency. Narrative texts provoke various emotions that follow the twists and turns of the story and culminate in a dramatic conclusion. Psalms and poetry are extremely sensate, while epistles are personal and instructive. Overall, our delivery should reflect these same emotional tones of the text we're preaching.

Beyond the genre, the subject of the passage should also inform our delivery. For instance, texts that are focused on hope and salvation should be declared with gospel joy and assurance. Lament and judgment topics should be preached with a sober and somber tone. Doctrinal or practical passages, which can sometimes be viewed as emotionally sterile, often have a pathos of exhortation, encouragement, or even earnestness, and we should preach them accordingly. While this may seem obvious, it's amazing how often preachers default to their typical communication style and are essentially tone deaf when it comes to a biblical text. But Spirit-empowered delivery occurs when we preach with the inspired passion expressed in the passage.

In addition to being determined by our zeal for the timeless truth and the inspired tone of the Scriptures, the Spirit's work in our delivery also operates through the authentic personality of the preacher. While style and emotion aren't synonymous with the work of the Spirit, they are aspects of our disposition that he uses. These elements are obviously

---

2   For a more thorough handling of issues related to the tone of the text and its implications for expository preaching, see Steven Smith, *Recapturing the Voice of God: Shaping Sermons Like Scripture* (Nashville: B&H, 2015).

secondary to the textual convictions and considerations, but they're still significant.

As pastors, we typically find ourselves in one of two extremes when it comes to our role in proclaiming God's word. Although most would never express it this way, some preachers operate as though they are the determining factor in whether the Lord works through the pulpit. This assumption is sometimes evident by superficial aspects like their stylish attire or larger-than-life personality. In more subtle ways, it can sneak up on all of us when we begin to operate like we're indispensable or when our pulpit persona doesn't resemble our everyday demeanor. This preacher pride is also revealed when we begin to focus on what we deserve, like a higher salary or more respect, or when we measure our success by church attendance, public response, or social media views. In essence, we become peddlers of God's word who preach for people to watch instead of worship, for them to be entertained instead of transformed, and to pacify our insecurities with compliments instead of praising the name of Jesus. We can be certain that the Spirit is not empowering our preaching when this is the case.

On the other end of the spectrum, many pastors want to completely disregard their role in the sermon. In genuine humility and with a sincere desire to not be a distraction or deterrent to God's work, they downplay their significance by stripping their delivery of any personal elements. But this discounts God's calling and his ability to use imperfect people as his instruments to accomplish his perfect plan. Similar to how the Spirit inspired the biblical writers and incorporated their personal style and story, he also desires to use us as preachers to proclaim his truth.

This doesn't mean that we are declaring new revelation or delivering an infallible message, but the Spirit does speak through us as we faithfully preach his inspired Scriptures. In doing so, he leverages our life as a corroborating testimony of the gospel, our imperfections as indicators that Jesus is the only perfect Savior, and our inadequacies as opportunities to demonstrate the sufficiency of his grace and power. Even more specific to each of us is the fact that the church we're called to serve, the people we preach to, the season of life we're in, and the surrounding circumstances in our community are all providentially orchestrated in a way that makes us God's chosen spokesman for a particular ministry assignment.

Overall, God's gracious desire to use us despite our imperfections is liberating! It frees us from the pressure of performing, the captivity of our insecurities, and the burden of expectations. Most importantly, it allows us to focus on being faithful to the text and to trust the Spirit to empower us as we preach with inspired passion and authentic personality. As a result, our spiritual leadership will prayerfully produce the same outcome for our people that Paul desired for the Corinthians—that our "faith might not rest in the wisdom of men but in the power of God" (1 Cor. 2:5).

### Spirit-Enabled Sermon Application

Up to this point, our focus has been on the essence of spiritual leadership as we facilitate the work of the Spirit through our ministry of the word. But the Spirit's role in our preparation and delivery must translate into the Spirit's work in the lives of our hearers. In partnership with the Spirit, sermon application may be the most definitive way that we exercise spiritual leadership from the pulpit.

Application is an intriguing subject in the field of homiletics. The responsibility of the preacher to identify practical implications and the degree of specificity are subjects of debate among scholars and practitioners. While there are nuances within the discussion, there are several reasons why we would contend that preachers are responsible to include some form of application in their sermons, especially as a crucial part of spiritual leadership.

First, Scripture is propositional revelation, meaning it discloses divine truth that requires a response. God's word is practical by nature, drawing a connection between the transfer of information and personal transformation. Scripture "is profitable for teaching, for reproof, for correction, and for training in righteousness," enabling God's people to become mature and complete (2 Tim. 3:16–17). From a hermeneutical standpoint, this means that the text has not been fully interpreted until it has been applied. From a homiletical standpoint, we would argue that a passage has not been fully expounded until it has been applied. Second, the prophetic nature of preaching as "exhortation" and "teaching" make it inherently applicable for those who hear (1 Tim. 4:13). Third, Scripture prescribes sermon application—implicitly by example and explicitly by directive. Nehemiah and the priests modeled it as they explained the Scriptures to the people of Israel and helped them understand and apply it (Neh. 8:1–8). Likewise, the command to "preach the word" includes a simultaneous charge to apply the text as we "reprove, rebuke, and exhort with complete patience and teaching" (2 Tim. 4:2).

Perhaps the most compelling impetus for including application in the sermon is our opportunity to cooperate with the Holy Spirit. Though some preachers avoid including application in deference to the Spirit, we actually have the responsibility (and privilege!) to participate in his work of applying the truth. Only the Spirit and the Scriptures have the power to change hearts, but as preachers of the word we are his delegated spokesmen, charged to communicate on his behalf.

There are two essential components of sermon application that cooperate with the specific aspects of the Spirit's work in the life of the listener. First, and most importantly, we must apply the Scriptures in a way that promotes spiritual growth. We faithfully preach the Scriptures because we are convinced that they function as a scalpel that cuts with power and precision in the human heart (Heb. 4:12). Still, "the word of God" is ultimately "the sword of the Spirit" (Eph. 6:17), and he wields it and operates in ways that we can't see or control. So our responsibility for application begins by preaching in a way that mirrors his work, "rightly handling the word of truth" with power and precision (2 Tim. 2:15).

In addition to being an instrument of the Spirit, the Scriptures are also a source of spiritual nourishment. Just as a newborn baby is nurtured and develops, the Bible enables us to "grow" in our faith (1 Pet. 2:2). Jesus himself affirmed that God's word is our spiritual sustenance

(Matt. 4:4) and the means by which we experience spiritual growth and sanctification (John 17:17). The ministry of the word is what Jesus had in mind after his resurrection when he repeatedly directed Peter to "feed my sheep" (John 21:15–17). Perhaps this is why Peter and the apostles were convinced that it was "not right that [they] should give up preaching the word of God to serve tables" (Acts 6:2). They ultimately delegated the responsibility to distribute the physical food while they focused on preparing the spiritual meals.

As pastors, we have the responsibility to provide the spiritual nourishment for our people and to "feed [the] sheep" a steady diet of God's word. But no matter how spiritually substantial our sermons are, our people will be malnourished if they don't learn to feed themselves throughout the week. This is one of the reasons why biblical exposition is essential for effective spiritual leadership. Our preaching should model for our people how to interpret and apply God's word so that they are equipped to consume it on their own, ensuring their spiritual health and growth.

Using Scripture, the Spirit's instrument and source of nourishment, we should complement his work by prescribing Spirit-enabled application. We have the responsibility to teach our people to devote themselves to good works (Titus 3:8), but spiritual growth doesn't occur by simply trying harder, doing more, or being better. It is the Spirit who actually changes hearts and produces spiritual fruit (Gal. 5:22–23). As we provide sermon application, we must be clear about this with our people. It's only through surrender and submission to the Spirit that we can experience freedom in Christ (Rom. 8:2), enjoy true "life and peace" (8:6), live a life that is pleasing to God (8:7–8), and have intimate fellowship with him (8:15–17). It's only through the Spirit that we can defeat sin (8:13), live with hope (8:23–25), and overcome life's hardships (8:35–37).

Even though the Spirit accomplishes the transforming work in our lives, spiritual growth isn't entirely passive. Like we do as preachers, our people must learn to cooperate with the work of the Spirit. This involves the second aspect of Spirit-empowered application—

in addition to promoting spiritual growth, our sermon application must provide spiritual guidance. One of the main aspects of the Spirit's role in our lives is his leadership. We mentioned previously the Spirit's role in "guid[ing]" us to understand the truth of Scripture (John 16:13). But his guidance is also a foundational aspect of his comprehensive work in directing our life (John 3:8), from our spiritual walk to our spiritual wisdom.

Throughout Scripture, our journey with the Lord is described as our "walk" with him. God walked with Adam (Gen. 3:8), Enoch, and Noah (Gen. 5:22; 6:9), and instructs all of his people throughout history to walk humbly with him according to his ways (Micah 6:8). In the New Testament, Jesus's most frequent invitation was "follow me" (Matt. 16:24), and John instructed believers to "walk in the same way in which [Jesus] walked" (1 John 2:6). Overall, the figurative language of walking communicates the ideas of direction, destination, purpose, and progress in our journeys.

While we are commanded "to walk in a manner worthy of the Lord" (Col. 1:10; Eph. 4:1), we must recognize that our ability to do so is also a work of the Spirit. This is why we're commanded to "walk by the Spirit" and "keep in step with the Spirit" (Gal. 5:16, 25). The Spirit's guidance includes direction and discernment in every area of our lives. As we prescribe application in our sermons, we must depend on the guidance of the Spirit to identify practical applications of the text for our people. These can include specific steps for them to take, relevant examples of the truth lived out, a biblical perspective for them to transform their thinking with, or a theological truth for them to embrace. Whatever practical form the text dictates, we must challenge them to be "led by the Spirit" (Rom. 8:14; cf. Gal. 5:18) as they walk according to the guiding light of God's word (Ps. 119:105) in their pursuit of Christlikeness.

As the Spirit guides their spiritual walk, he also leads them with spiritual wisdom. While biblical knowledge informs the intellect, wisdom instructs the will and applies the truth of God's word. Wisdom is inherently practical and is made evident by works that reflect godly understanding (James 3:13). And wisdom from the Lord is distinguished from earthly wisdom that is "unspiritual" and displays itself in selfishness and "every vile practice" (James 3:15–16). God's wisdom is infinitely superior (1 Cor. 1:19–25) and is manifested in good fruits and righteous behavior (James 3:17–18).

Thus, Spirit-empowered application seeks to provide guidance for our people with spiritual wisdom as they live according to the Scriptures. Positionally, believers have access to godly understanding through their relationship with Christ, who is the source of "all the treasures of wisdom and knowledge" (Col. 2:3). Practically, believers can live according to this wisdom because they have been given "the Spirit of wisdom" (Eph. 1:17) who translates their positional status in Christ into practical behavior and application.

Overall, our responsibility as preachers is to cooperate in the Spirit's work by identifying the practical precepts from our preaching passage for our people. At its most basic level this means that we help them connect the dots from the theological and doctrinal truths of the text to the practical implications for their lives. It's not always complex or profound, but as we press the truth of God's word into their hearts, we collaborate with the Spirit by identifying areas and aspects of their lives that need spiritual growth and guidance. In doing so, we exert spiritual leadership through Spirit-empowered application that works according to the divine instrument of his word to provide nourishment and inform their walk with wisdom.

Just as the previous aspects of the Spirit's role in our sermon preparation and delivery were activated through prayer, our ability to deliver Spirit-enabled application also depends on prayer. Paul's intercession for the Colossians combined the applicational concepts of growth and guidance along with the practical aspects of their spiritual walk and wisdom. He prayed that they "may *be filled with the knowledge of his will* in all spiritual *wisdom and understanding,* so as to *walk* in a manner worthy of the Lord" as they continued to grow in their knowledge of God and live in a manner "fully pleasing to him" (Col. 1:9–10). In the same way, we must pray for God's wisdom and understanding as we identify applications for our people, and we must pray for the Spirit to enable them to apply it to their lives.

## Conclusion

Overall, the spiritual leadership a pastor provides from the pulpit occurs on several levels. On a personal level, it begins with our own growth that results from our encounter with God's Spirit in our personal study and sermon preparation. When we study God's word, we learn to listen to the voice of the Spirit in the text because we are abiding in his presence and experiencing his transforming power. As we proclaim God's word, we are called to reflect his glory and display a spiritual maturity for his people that embodies the truth of the text we're preaching and invites them to further pursue Christ in their own personal relationship with him.

On a Scriptural level, our exposition of the text should model sound interpretative principles for God's people to implement in their own devotional study of God's word. Our practical applications of the text should also exhort them toward spiritual growth and godliness as they submit themselves to Scripture through the power of the Spirit. This will cultivate a community of faith that loves God's word and submits to its authority, which will in turn promote a healthy body of Christ that progresses toward maturity.

Spiritual leadership also occurs on the corporate level as we preach to the gathered community of faith and the Spirit works among the collective body of believers. Through the public ministry of the word, the spots and wrinkles are rinsed and removed from the bride of Christ by "the washing of water with the word" so that she might become "holy and without blemish" (Eph. 5:26–27). When we faithfully preach God's word and call our people to walk in humility, gentleness, patience, and love, it promotes the "unity of the Spirit in the bond of peace" (Eph. 4:2–3).

Ultimately, when we devote ourselves to Spirit-encountered sermon preparation, Spirit-empowered sermon delivery, and Spirit-enabled sermon application, we can exert spiritual leadership that effectively shepherds God's people from the pulpit. But, as we have seen in each section of this chapter, none of this can occur without undergirding every aspect of our preaching with Spirit-dependent prayer. This ensures that whatever spiritual leadership we exhibit, it's the result of the Spirit's leadership in our lives.

3

# Strategic Leadership from the Pulpit

*With upright heart he shepherded them and*
*guided them with his skillful hand.*

PSALM 78:72

AN INTERVIEWER ONCE ASKED Haddon Robinson—the great preacher and teacher of preaching—how preachers should speak about situations not addressed directly in the biblical text. Robinson's response was surprising: "It doesn't really help listeners to say, 'God doesn't speak to your situation. . . . Sometimes, though, I think a preacher would do a congregation well to say that. It's instructive that some things we spend time praying about have so little kingdom dimension to them." The interviewer continued, "Are preachers today more likely to apply a passage a certain way than would preachers of a generation ago?" Robinson replied, "Today, what's prevalent is specific application. In the past, the application would have been more general—to trust God and give him glory. Today, preaching deals with how to have a happy marriage, how to bring up your children, how to deal with stress."[1]

Herein lies the rub in the relationship between pastoral preaching and strategic leadership. There are an infinite number of issues that

---

1   Haddon Robinson, "The Heresy of Application," *Leadership* (Fall 1997): 24.

vie for the pastor's attention in his extremely limited and valuable preaching time with his people. Some of those issues are biblical issues, ones that God addresses directly in his word. Examples of this would include creation, sin, righteousness, holiness, the gospel, the return of Christ, heaven, hell, and disciple making. Other issues are extra-biblical because Scripture doesn't address them directly.[2] On a personal level, this might include raising a special needs child or planning for retirement. On a congregational level, it might be launching a capital fundraising campaign, adopting a neighboring church to revitalize, or initiating a new ministry of foster care. On a cultural level, it might be addressing the transgender debate or the increase of violence in our society.

This tension between biblical and extra-biblical issues creates a dilemma for pastors who obviously want to help their people and lead them to worthy endeavors. How, then, does a pastor steward his pulpit to meet the tension between faithful exposition of God's word and strategic leadership of his congregation? Doing this requires assessing the challenge we're up against, aiming for our God-given goal in pastoral ministry, and rightly applying the principles of God's word to our particular ministry context.

## Assessing the Problem

Successfully navigating the tension between faithful preaching and strategic pastoral leadership begins with understanding why it's such a challenge in the first place. While there are numerous reasons that pastors fall in the ditch on one side or the other of their leadership journey, four particular hurdles stand out.

### Limited Facetime

One of the reasons many pastors tend to fall into one ditch or the other is because they know they only have so much time with their people

---

2   We prefer to use the term "extra-biblical" instead of "unbiblical" or "non-biblical" because many issues not explicitly addressed in Scripture are morally neutral or good rather than heretical or evil.

as a group. And the sermon obviously comprises the largest amount of airtime for pastors to be with the entire congregation, look them in the eyes, and lead them where they need to go. Furthermore, this amount of time has been abbreviated even more through the years as churches have evolved (or devolved) toward ministry schedules that include only one corporate gathering each week. Abbreviated schedules in many churches have also led to shorter amounts of time being allotted for the sermon. Most pastors believe they are responsible for both feeding their flocks spiritually and guiding them practically. They know that both are involved in leading, equipping, and mobilizing their local church to accomplish the Great Commission in their respective context. But when they face the reality of having only so much time when their people gather as a group for worship, the challenge of how to spend that time is magnified.

### Complexity of the Church

Another challenge to the dual responsibilities of Bible preaching and strategic leadership is the complexity of church programming and scheduling, especially in many Western churches. We have come a long way from the simplicity of the house church model that characterized most of the New Testament congregations. Let's face it—many churches are busy! And they're busy with good stuff. Small groups, age-specific programs, discipleship initiatives, stewardship campaigns, support groups, men's and women's ministries, and a plethora of special events all vie for time in the church's weekly schedules. Additionally, our facilities and properties are more complex than they used to be. We have more buildings, and we have bigger buildings, whether owned or leased. In addition to this, most churches own property. All of these facilities require fundraising campaigns and maintenance programs, which in turn demand more promotion. Further, ministry leaders, staff, congregations, and even pastors themselves feel like the pastoral voice is the most influential when it comes to championing a given cause, which puts additional pressure on pastors regarding how they spend their pulpit time.

## Redefinition of the Pastorate

Another challenge facing pastors today is the subtle and gradual re-definition of the pastor's role. In the New Testament, the word "pastor" (*poimen*) means "shepherd," one whose main responsibilities are to feed and protect the sheep. Specifically in the pastoral epistles, both of those tasks are carried out primarily through the preaching and teaching of God's word (see 1 Tim. 1:3–4; 3:2; 4:6–7, 13–16; 5:17–18; 6:3–5, 20–21; 2 Tim. 1:6–8, 13–14; 2:1–2, 8–9, 14–16; 3:14–17; 4:1–5; Titus 1:7–14; 2:1, 15).[3] Through the years, however, the idea of being a shepherd has come to mean "pastoral care," as differentiated from preaching and teaching. Many Christians still draw a distinction between being a good pastor and being a good preacher. Today, the perception of the pastor has gravitated even further away from its original meaning. Many pastors and churches see the pastor's primary task not as preaching or pastoral care but as leadership. The overabundance of books, courses, assessments, and conferences on leadership gives testimony to our infatuation with the subject. It's not hard to see why many pastors are tempted to view their preaching time as more of a leadership platform than dispensing God's word.

## False Dichotomy

All the above challenges (and more!) have contributed to creating a false dichotomy in many pastors' minds between preaching and strategic leadership. We simply want to believe that they're mutually exclusive, an either-or situation instead of a both-and. And when these two pastoral responsibilities are separated, it's easy to feel like we must choose between using the pulpit for preaching the Bible or leading our people to do the work of the church. Sadly, the unintended consequence of such a contrast ends up—more often than not—with pastors neglecting the former and featuring the latter, largely due to the sway of the aforementioned challenges.

3   Jerry Vines and Jim Shaddix, *Power in the Pulpit: How to Prepare and Deliver Expository Sermons*, rev. ed. (Chicago: Moody, 2017), 84–85.

These things ought not to be, to say the least. Their reality, however, is part of what compels us to address the need for expositional leadership. It's true that pastors preach and lead in varying contexts made up of diverse people groups that are characterized by a seemingly infinite number of variables. But pastoral sermons—grounded in and driven by the authoritative meaning of the divine author as expressed through the biblical writers—can and should be developed and directed to those specific situations, connected to particular people, and pastorally applied to certain churches. Contextualization and mobilization for our respective spiritual communities can be accomplished through faithful exposition if we cast vision and extend challenges that are dictated by what God says, not what we've dreamed up for our ministries. In fact, when our preaching is driven by what God says in his word, we can still highlight points of emphasis, support congregational initiatives, and encourage collaborative efforts to accomplish his mission and fulfill his will for our local body of believers.

## Aiming for the Prize

Providing strategic leadership for a congregation through preaching must always begin with the destination in mind. Remember, leadership implies a destination. We don't just lead; we lead *somewhere*. And that unique *somewhere* of pastoral leadership must determine strategic leadership. Overall, the Bible describes God's destination for his people in several ways. We first introduced this in chapter 1 when we discussed the pastor's goal of godliness for his people. However, one of the apostle Paul's more picturesque descriptions is the idea of a prize. He claimed, "I press on toward the goal for the prize of the upward call of God in Christ Jesus" (Phil. 3:14). Paul had given up everything in order that he might "know [Christ] and the power of his resurrection, and may share his sufferings, becoming like him in his death, that by any means possible [he] may attain the resurrection from the dead" (Phil. 3:10–11).

For Paul, the greatest attainment one could aspire to was knowing Christ fully and experiencing perfect communion with him. Jesus Christ demonstrated obedience to the point of death as well as resurrection to new life, and Paul wanted both for himself and his readers. That's where pastors should be leading people first and foremost. Whether we're giving strategic leadership to our people is determined by whether we're strategically leading them to that prize. So what does that prize look like, and how do we strategically lead our people to it in our preaching?

## Image Re-Creation

Overall, the pursuit of the prize of knowing Christ and becoming like him is equivalent to the biblical concept of being spiritually formed into Christ's image. From eternity past, God ordained this to be his highest purpose: "Those whom he foreknew he also predestined to be conformed to the image of his Son, in order that he might be the firstborn among many brothers" (Rom. 8:29). The grand story of the Bible describes this purpose in terms of creation and re-creation. The Bible literally begins and ends with these themes. It begins with the creation of heaven and earth and the creation of humanity in God's image (Gen. 1). It ends with the re-creation of heaven and earth and the re-creation of humanity into God's image (Rev. 21–22). And everything in between is the story of how sin marred God's creation but he re-created it through Jesus Christ (e.g., Ps. 17:15; Rom. 8:29–30; 2 Cor. 3:18; 4:16; Gal. 4:19; Phil. 3:21; Col. 3:10; 1 John 3:2; 2 Pet. 1:3–4). That's the gospel! That's the story of the Bible.[4]

Strategic leadership of God's people, then, takes place when pastors foster the re-creation God ordained from eternity past. The pastor's number one goal in his preaching should be to foster that re-creative process in people's lives. We have no business leading them to catch our vision for church growth or buy into our flashy mission statement if we're not first leading them to look more and more like Jesus. When we evaluate the previous year, we need to be assessing whether our people look more like Jesus today than they did last year. And

---

4    For a more detailed treatment of creation and re-creation as God's agenda in the Bible, see Jim Shaddix, *The Passion-Driven Sermon: Changing the Way Pastors Preach and Congregations Listen* (Nashville: B&H, 2003), 66–69.

when we plan for the coming church calendar, our first and highest goal ought to be to lead people to know Jesus more and bear a closer resemblance to him.

## Scripture Transformation

The Bible is not silent on how this re-creative process comes about. In addition to unfolding the gospel story, Scripture also claims that its truth is the primary tool the Holy Spirit uses to transform people into Christ's image, an idea we introduced in the previous chapter (see John 17:17; Acts 20:32; Rom. 10:17; 2 Tim. 3:14–17; James 1:21; 1 Pet. 1:22–2:2). This is one of the main reasons it's imperative for preachers to interpret each text rightly, find the Spirit's intended meaning in each passage, and proclaim it accordingly. The Bible's supernatural power to bring about God's purpose of re-creation is tied to what God inspired it to say. Within the context of hearing and responding to God's voice, people are shaped into the *imago Dei* through the work of God's Spirit. In this manner, God's people, "with unveiled face, beholding the glory of the Lord, are being transformed into the same image from one degree of glory to another. For this comes from the Lord who is the Spirit" (2 Cor. 3:18).

In addition to the ideas of godliness and creation (or re-creation), the apostle Paul also uses the concept of righteousness to describe Scripture's effect on those who hear and receive it. He reminded his young protégé pastor Timothy that "all Scripture is breathed out by God and profitable for teaching, for reproof, for correction, and for training in righteousness, that the man of God may be complete, equipped for every good work" (2 Tim. 3:16–17). Paul believed Scripture was sufficient for Timothy to strategically lead himself and his people where they needed to go, namely to "righteousness" (2 Tim. 3:16). In fact, using Holy Scripture to produce righteousness in Timothy's people was so important to Paul that he appealed to the judging eye of the Lord Jesus Christ for accountability: "I charge you in the presence of God and of Christ Jesus, who is to judge the living and the dead, and by his appearing and his kingdom" (2 Tim. 4:1). Paul knew that Jesus was serious about his preachers doing what is necessary for his people to be shaped in righteousness, "to put on the new self, created after the likeness of God in true righteousness and holiness" (Eph. 4:24).

Timothy's mentor also knew the young pastor would face never-ending temptation to preach to his congregants about lesser things and only lead them to places that they preferred to go. So, he told Timothy to

> preach the word; be ready in season and out of season; reprove, rebuke, and exhort, with complete patience and teaching. For the time is coming when people will not endure sound teaching, but having itching ears they will accumulate for themselves teachers to suit their own passions, and will turn away from listening to the truth and wander off into myths. (2 Tim. 4:2–4)

Well, that time has long since arrived. Contemporary pastors face this temptation every week. Many congregations have been groomed to expect the sermon to be a clinic of practical advice or a presentation on ministry vision. And they expect as much because their pastors have bought into a redefinition of preaching that is more concerned with large group counseling and program promotion than it is with transformation into righteousness.

### Systematic Exposition

The prize of Christlikeness fostered by the supernatural agent of biblical truth means that simple, faithful Bible exposition is the most strategic leadership a pastor can give his people through his preaching. Preachers today have sixty-six books of God's truth that comprise the most powerful agent in the universe and contain the only hope of humanity. We don't live under the pressure of coming up with our own material and spinning it as the words of God. We don't have to cast our own visions or concoct our own dreams for our people that are distinct from or loosely connected to what God says in the Bible. Rather, pastors can, should, and must discover and declare what God says by doing

Spirit-empowered exposition of the Bible. Helping people hear and obey God's truth is strategic leadership of the highest order.

In light of this reality, the simplest and best way we can communicate God's truth is by doing systematic exposition, which entails preaching through books of the Bible or extended portions contained within them. Going through sections of the Bible systematically is not the only way pastors preach, but it ought to be their bread and butter. Congregations need a steady diet of biblical exposition where their pastors simply take what God has said, interpret it in its context, explain it to them, and apply it to their lives. Faithful pastoral leadership is demonstrated most compellingly when we lead our people to hear God's voice, and since his voice rings clear all the way from Genesis to Revelation, preaching through books of the Bible positions our people to clearly hear that voice.

Systematic exposition is strategic preaching and leadership at its best. What God has said and is saying to everyone through his inspired Scripture is more important than any vision, plan, program, or goal we come up with for our respective congregations. And as we expound the Bible purposefully, we'll be amazed at the supernatural way the Holy Spirit connects it to our contemporary culture, to our particular parish, and to the people we pastor. Systematic exposition done well always proves to be timely and relevant because God supernaturally speaks to his people.

*Passage Inquisition*

As a pastor purposefully works through Bible passages, one of the most practical ways he can preach strategically for re-creation is to ask two questions of every biblical text. First, Is there anything in this text that speaks to how sin has marred the image of God in people? Bryan Chapell helps us think about this question by encouraging preachers to look for the "Fallen Condition Focus" (FCF) in every passage. He defines this as "the mutual human condition that contemporary persons share with those to or about whom the text was written that requires the grace of the passage for God's people to glorify and enjoy him."[5] When we identify such a condition in the passage, we've located something that reflects a breach in the image of God, something only the gospel can fix.

A second question preachers should ask is, Is there anything in this text that displays or demonstrates the image of Christ? In *Privilege the Text!*, Abraham Kuruvilla argues for "christiconic interpretation that sees each pericope of Scripture portraying a facet of the canonical image of Christ. God's goal for his children is that they be conformed to this image . . . of his Son (Rom. 8:29)."[6] In every passage, the preacher can seek to determine what facets might be present, facets that will only be realized in people's life through the gospel.

Preaching pastors desperately need to be reoriented to God's purpose in the Bible of re-creating people into his image in Jesus Christ. Every time a pastor opens the Bible, interprets it rightly, and proclaims it to his people in the power of the Holy Spirit, he supports the Spirit's work of regenerating God's people. He exposes them to the only thing that can shape them in godliness and righteousness. Such is pastoral leadership in its best and most important form. Even if we never mention the vision or program that's unique to our particular congregation, we're strategically leading our people to the most important place we can lead them—to the prize of knowing Jesus—by simply exposing them to God's truth and compelling them to embrace it.

### Applying the Passage

While the pastor primarily leads through faithful Bible exposition, he also is tasked with other leadership responsibilities that don't always fit as neatly into the intended meaning of specific texts of Scripture. This reality creates a dilemma for many pastors. Should the pulpit be silent on extra-biblical subjects simply because the Bible doesn't speak

---

5   Bryan Chapell, *Christ-Centered Preaching: Redeeming the Expository Sermon*, 3rd ed. (Grand Rapids, MI: Baker, 2018), 47.

6   Abraham Kuruvilla, *Privilege the Text!: A Theological Hermeneutic for Preaching* (Chicago: Moody, 2013), 29. Though we wouldn't necessarily embrace the entirety of Kuruvilla's hermeneutical approach, some of his assertions about the image of Christ throughout Scripture can be adapted to preaching for spiritual formation.

to them directly? Should equal preaching time be given to addressing biblical and extra-biblical subjects? This struggle involves ditches on both sides of this road of shepherding.

The answer to this dilemma can be found in the nature and breadth of sermon application. As noted in the previous chapter, we depend on the Holy Spirit to enable both spiritual growth and guidance in the application process. When we partner with the Spirit in this endeavor, it's possible for us to incorporate strategic leadership on extra-biblical subjects into our biblical preaching and to do so with integrity. Following are some important steps to accomplishing this task.

*Begin with Some Basics*

Many pastors never think critically about the quandary they face when it comes to how they steward their preaching time. When that happens, they often end up forcing congregational and contextual issues into their sermonizing by spiritualizing God's word and mis-using it in other ways. They try to fit a square peg of some pastoral leadership responsibilities into the round hole of what God is actually saying in the biblical text. Before engaging in such hermeneutical and homiletical gymnastics, there are some basic guidelines every pastor ought to consider.

First, don't overlook the obvious. Whenever you're considering preaching a sermon or a series that's intended to strategically lead your congregation to a particular end, be sure that you don't overlook the possibility that God may actually address your subject or initiative as part of his agenda in Scripture. The Bible does speak directly to so many major life issues as they relate to God's redemptive plan and re-creation in Christ's image. For example, it addresses human identity, the problem of evil, the purpose of life, the future, guilt, love, marriage, family, death, and eternity. It also addresses congregational issues like local and global disciple making, church multiplication, missional stewardship, shared ministry, community, unity, hospitality, restoration, and discipline.

So always start by asking and answering the quintessential question, Did God address this subject directly? If he did, then you're good to go! If the subject on your heart for your people relates to the redemption of humanity through the gospel and the transformation of individuals into Christlikeness as unfolded in the biblical narrative, then your task of wedding together your preaching and leading has basically been done for you by the Spirit's work of inspiration in the Bible. Your agenda is a biblical issue, not an extra-biblical one. You simply need to identify the passages where that subject is addressed, interpret them in their context, develop your sermon or series based on one or more of them, and challenge your people through faithful Bible exposition.

Second, consider other communication channels. Sometimes—after honest assessment—the pastor has to come face-to-face with the fact that the answer to that quintessential question is no because the Bible doesn't directly address the burden or practical vision he has for his people. We've already acknowledged that the Bible's agenda is to foster re-creation in Christ Jesus, not address every subject or answer every question. Thus, sometimes the pastor finds himself trying to shepherd his people to something that's good and helpful but doesn't necessarily have a biblical passage dedicated to it. In other words, while God's redemptive plan is the pastor's underlying motive, the particular thing he wants to challenge his people to do is either a secondary issue in the biblical text or just one of many possible applications. When you find yourself at this place, then you've got more work to do when it comes to leading your people. But don't immediately assume that the only way to provide that leadership is to relegate your precious preaching time to casting visions, promoting programs, or teaching people life skills.

While the sermon is the pastor's most consistent and influential leadership platform, it's not the only method he has for communicating with his people. Pastor, don't ever forget that you have other mediums through which you can strategically lead your congregation. When the time comes to take your congregation in a new direction or challenge them to achieve a new goal, take advantage of all relevant means of communication you have outside the pulpit, including social media, email blitzes, blogs, vlogs, website blurbs, and church newsletter columns. You can also use brief presentations during worship gatherings, members' meetings, and special assemblies to introduce or provide updates related to ministry emphases and initiatives. Printed materials that are mailed to church members or dispersed at worship gatherings can also be used to communicate relevant information. The point is that you don't have to feel pressured to surrender your pulpit time to addressing issues that the Bible doesn't address. There are other avenues through which you can provide practical leadership.

*Reorder the Study Routine*

As we've already acknowledged, it is possible—and sometimes needful—for pastors to address situational and contextual issues that are not directly addressed in Scripture while at the same time remaining faithful to the biblical text. But doing so requires the expositor to judiciously reorder some aspects of the study and preparation process that he's normally accustomed to doing, particularly the steps taken to determine how the truth of the passage relates to his congregation.

Here's what we mean. Many expositors have found it helpful to think about application in terms of a continuum.[7] After exegeting the text and finding the Holy Spirit's intended meaning, they seek to avoid spiritualizing the passage by identifying its theological implications. Instead, they probe the text to determine what it teaches us about God, humanity, Christ, and the gospel. Once they've identified the theological implications of the passage, they then move to determining the timeless truth that grows out of its theology, principles that are true for all people throughout history. Then and only then do they begin to ask how the passage applies specifically and practically to their particular people in their specific context. In other words, practical application should be driven and fenced in by the

---

7   For a fuller discussion of using the application continuum, see Vines and Shaddix, *Power in the Pulpit*, 174–80, 224–26.

theology of the text and the timeless truth that grows out of that theology. We can illustrate the movement like this (see figure below):

Passage  →  Theological  →  Timeless  →  Practical
exegesis      implications      truth         application

When our starting point, however, is something specific to our context and not directly addressed in the Bible, all hope is not lost in preaching an expositional sermon as part of our effort to strategically lead our people to a particular place. What we can do (albeit with great fear and trepidation) is slightly reorder the study process as follows (see figure below):

Practical  →  Theological  →  Passage  →  Timeless
application    implications      exegesis      truth

When we have an extra-biblical goal, vision, or endeavor we want to lead our people to—something that's not directly addressed in the Bible—we're obviously starting with practical application in our minds (although we don't really have anything to apply yet!). Some preachers might call such an approach a topical-theological-textual method of developing a message.

Needless to say, this is dangerous ground on which preachers must tread carefully. If we're not particularly vigilant at this point, we will end up spiritualizing or proof texting a Bible passage and making God say something that he didn't actually say. So, how does the preacher navigate these tumultuous waters of reordering his study routine? Consider the following steps.

First, determine the theological implications. It's crucial to position your extra-biblical topic or project into the framework of the Bible's agenda by determining the theology that undergirds it. To do so, you might ask some probing questions like these: How might the fallen nature of humanity hinder this endeavor? What is it about the image of God in Christ that will be needed for this goal to be accomplished? How does the place you want to lead your people to relate to making disciples and advancing the gospel among the nations? Probe your topic honestly and diligently to determine what doctrinal issues are at play.

Second, identify a corresponding Bible passage. Once you've processed the theological tenets that relate to your particular extra-biblical goal, locate some biblical texts that correspond to those tenets. What passages speak directly to the doctrines you identified? What passages make significant contributions to the theological issues that relate to your topic? In addition to leaning on your own knowledge of Scripture at this point, you may want to consult some good systematic theology and biblical theology resources to help you choose corresponding texts well. Once you've identified and processed those passages, choose the passage that most clearly informs one or more of your theological implications as your preaching text.

Third, exegete the passage objectively. Once you've identified a relevant Bible text, set your extra-biblical agenda or topic aside temporarily and study the Bible passage. Using the grammatical-historical-theological hermeneutical approach to reduce subjectivity, study and interpret your passage just as you would in the normal course of your expositional process. Be extremely careful to not allow your extra-biblical topic to skew your understanding of what the Holy Spirit was intending to say in the text when he inspired it. You want to be sure to exegete his meaning out of the text, not eisegete your extra-biblical agenda into it. Finish by summarizing your interpretation in one sentence that expresses the main idea of the text.

Fourth, find the timeless principles in the passage. Once you've studied your text and interpreted it correctly, there's still important work to do that paves the way for good and right sermon application to your extra-biblical topic. You need to determine the application of your passage for contemporary listeners by finding one or more timeless principles. Harold Freeman calls this "principlization."[8] Haddon Robinson describes it in terms of climbing the "ladder of abstraction" from the historical context of the passage to its

8    Harold Freeman, *Variety in Biblical Preaching* (Fort Worth, TX: Scripta, 1994), 41.

application for contemporary audiences.[9] Basically, this process involves stripping the passage of things that were specific to its biblical culture and identifying its timeless truth. Sometimes the significance of the text is the same today as it was then. But other times the meaning must be converted into a principle that is relevant for contemporary audiences.

Fifth, establish the connections with your extra-biblical topic. At this point in your study, you have a number of working parts: (1) an extra-biblical topic you want to address with your people, (2) some theological tenets that undergird that topic, (3) a relevant biblical text that informs those theological tenets, (4) a main idea statement that reflects the Holy Spirit's intended meaning of that text, and (5) at least one timeless principle that connects that meaning to the contemporary context. With all those elements in hand, spend some time processing the relationships between them, particularly between your extra-biblical topic and the others. How is the theology of your text critical for making your topic fruitful and God-honoring? How does the Holy Spirit's intent in the text speak to your topic? How is the timeless truth in your text demonstrated through your topic?

Before we move on, it might be helpful to consider a hypothetical example. Suppose a pastor felt the need to lead his expanding congregation to revamp their existing Bible teaching ministry. Groups that historically were just large group Bible teaching venues would now be multiplied into smaller groups of ten to fifteen people that would expand their responsibilities to include intentional member care. While the New Testament doesn't really mandate member care and Bible teaching through groups of a particular size, the approach certainly could have practical merit, especially in growing congregations. One theological implication of such an endeavor is the concept of shared ministry. The pastor may thus identify Ephesians 4:1–16 as a biblical text that, in part, addresses the every-member ministry of the church. When he exegetes the passage objectively, he finds the main idea of

---

9   Robinson, "The Heresy of Application," 23.

the text to be something akin to, "Believers should conduct themselves in accordance with their calling as one body that is being shaped into Christ's image." One of the timeless principles that issues forth from this proposition is that Christ's church is to be shaped into his image partly through the equipping of every believer to do the work of gospel ministry. Further, one connection of this principle to the pastor's vision is that small group leaders can be equipped to help shepherd Christ's body through both Bible teaching and pastoral care.

### Preach the Scripture's Principle

After you've carefully gone through the process above, you should have what you need to prepare and preach a sermon or series of sermons that will assist in strategically leading your people to a desired destination. The key at this point is keeping your priorities straight—you must first preach the principle of the passage and then make application to your extra-biblical issue instead of first preaching your extra-biblical issue and thereby forcing unbiblical principles onto your text. There is a difference between the two. The former allows you to maintain the integrity of the sermon and your role as a preacher. The latter hijacks the biblical text and uses it to manipulate your people.

Here are a couple of guidelines for staying on the high road of preaching the principle in your text instead of the application of your text. First, distinguish the principle from the implications. As pastors, we must always be cognizant of the fact that people hear everything we say in our sermons as coming from God. Because of our authority as pastors and the fact that we're reading from God's word, they hear it all as, "Thus says the Lord." Therefore it is absolutely essential that when we're drawing implications from a passage in our sermons, we distinguish these implications from the binding principle in our passage. Robinson is helpful at this point:

> Implications may be necessary, probable, possible, improbable, or impossible. For example, a *necessary* implication of "You shall not commit adultery" is you cannot have a sexual relationship with a

person who is not your spouse. A *probable* implication is you ought to be very careful of strong bonding friendships with a person who is not your spouse. A *possible* implication is you ought not travel regularly to conventions or other places with a person who is not your spouse. An *improbable* conclusion is you should not at any time have lunch with someone who is not your spouse. An *impossible* implication is you ought not have dinner with another couple because you are at the same table with a person who is not your spouse.[10]

Robinson concludes, "Too often preachers give to a possible implication all the authority of a necessary implication, which is at the level of obedience. Only with necessary implications can you preach, 'Thus says the Lord.'"[11]

This reality is especially true when you're attempting to use your preaching ministry to lead your people to something that is essentially extra-biblical, something God doesn't address directly in the Bible. The principle that articulates the intent of your passage is the only "Thus says the Lord" you have and, therefore, the only thing that's necessarily binding on your people. In the hypothetical example we mentioned earlier, the "Thus says the Lord" is the instruction for believers to live out their calling by being equipped to serve in gospel ministry as part of their re-creation into Christ's image. The initiative for the local church to be organized into small groups for Bible study and congregational care is the extra-biblical program. It's just a possible—maybe probable—implication of that principle at best. And the pastor must be honest with his people and make that distinction for them during his sermon. He must prioritize the principle in his passage when he preaches; he must feature it to his people and highlight it above all else. If he reverses the emphasis and features his program, he'll be exhorting his people with something that has absolutely no ability to change their lives.

---

10   Robinson, "The Heresy of Application," 25–26.
11   Robinson, "The Heresy of Application," 26.

The second guideline is to exhort your people to obey the principle. It's not enough to distinguish the principle of your text from the implication for your agenda; you must also compel your people to obey the principle more than you compel them to embrace your agenda. When Paul charged Timothy to devote himself "to the public reading of Scripture, to exhortation, to teaching" (1 Tim. 4:13), he wasn't merely offering suggestions—he was commanding the young pastor to accomplish certain critical tasks in his preaching, and one of those nonnegotiables was "exhortation." This word specifically speaks of moral instruction that appeals to the will.[12] It involves challenging people to apply God's word and warning them to obey it.[13] It's a sincere and persuasive appeal, plea, encouragement, or invitation for people to say yes to the biblical principle that's being explained to them and applied to their lives.

Sincere exhortation is one of the many species of application that leaders use to compel people to follow them. When Paul said, "Be imitators of me, as I am of Christ" (1 Cor. 11:1), he was compelling people to follow him. We're not really leading people if we don't say to them, "Come, follow me." Exhortation leads and motivates people to demonstrate life transformation through obedience. As a shepherd-leader, you must sincerely and passionately appeal to people to render a positive verdict about the principle that's being proclaimed. And it's perfectly fine to call them to embrace an extrabiblical aspect as a worthy way to demonstrate their obedience. In fact, they will be more likely to follow you to your extra-biblical destination if they are persuaded to embrace what God is saying in the text.

## Conclusion

We've all heard popular religious sayings that sound really good on the surface but actually aren't true. For example, Leonard Ravenhill

---

12  Thomas D. Lea and Hayne P. Griffin, *1, 2 Timothy, Titus*, The New American Commentary (Nashville: B&H, 1992), 138.

13  John F. MacArthur, *1 Timothy* (Chicago: Moody, 1995), 176.

questions why "someone now warns us lest we become so heavenly minded that we are of no earthly use."[14] The assertion sounds like relevant practical theology, but it flies in the face of the apostle Paul's exhortation in Colossians 3:1–2 to "seek the things that are above, where Christ is, seated at the right hand of God. Set your minds on things that are above, not on things that are on earth." Therefore, concerning this misunderstanding, Ravenhill declares, "Brother, this generation of believers is not, by and large, suffering from such a complex! The brutal, soul-shaking truth is that we are so earthly minded we are of no heavenly use."[15]

Verbalized or not, similar untruths are embraced and championed when it comes to preaching and leadership. Some pastors are said to be so spiritually minded that they're no practical good. These shepherds fatten their congregations with Bible knowledge without ever connecting that knowledge to the specifics of their congregational journey. They preach deep sermons but provide shallow leadership. Still other pastors are accused of being so practically minded that they're no spiritual good. These guys gravitate to the other end of the spectrum by spending their preaching time casting temporal visions, rallying the troops around ministry programs, and promoting contextualized core values.

Neither of these exaggerated claims are entirely true, however. In pastoral preaching, if we're truly spiritually minded, we will be helpful to others in practical ways. And if we're helping them in practical ways, we'll probably be helping them in spiritual ways. To demonstrate these virtues in the marriage of our preaching and leadership, pastors must be cognizant of some of the forces that pressure us to be one or the other. We must also remain unapologetically committed to the ultimate goal of leading our people to Christlikeness through the exposition of Scripture. Finally, pastors must be disciplined to preach the Holy Spirit's meaning and intent in every passage instead

14   Leonard Ravenhill, *Why Revival Tarries* (Minneapolis: Bethany House, 1987), 29.
15   Ravenhill, *Why Revival Tarries*, 29–30.

of overshadowing those things with their extra-biblical agendas. When we submit our extra-biblical agendas as humble servants to the "Thus says the Lord" of Holy Scripture, we will lead our people in the most strategic way possible.

4

# Servant Leadership from the Pulpit

*For what we proclaim is not ourselves, but Jesus Christ as*
*Lord, with ourselves as your servants for Jesus' sake.*

2 CORINTHIANS 4:5

ANY DISCUSSION ABOUT BIBLICAL LEADERSHIP, including shepherding God's people from the pulpit, must be predicated on the concept of servant leadership. According to Scripture, service is not just an example or one of many ways we can influence others; rather, it defines leadership. In fact, to call it "servant leadership" could be considered redundant! Jesus clearly described leadership as service in his kingdom and—as the master teacher—he didn't just explain the concept but also embodied it in his life and ministry.

Overall, Jesus most clearly defined servant leadership when his disciples were arguing and posturing for places of influence and authority (Mark 10:35–41). He rebuked them and corrected their understanding of leadership by differentiating it from the culture's definition. As he explained, the world measures it by "rulers" who "lord it over" others, and they define greatness by how they "exercise authority over them" (Mark 10:42). But Jesus elevated servanthood as the true mark of leadership and challenged his followers to become "great" and "first" by becoming "lowly" and "last" (Mark 10:43–44).

After all, Jesus himself did not come "to be served but to serve" (Mark 10:45).

In addition to defining servant leadership for his disciples, Jesus also modeled it. His entire life and ministry exemplified what it looked like to avail yourself to others. Whether it was a small band of brothers intruding on behalf of their paralytic friend (Matt. 9:1–8), a religious official whose daughter was dying (Matt. 9:18–26), a self-conscious woman with a shameful secret who simply sought to touch his garment (Matt. 9:20–22), or two desperate blind men pleading for mercy (Matt. 9:27–31), Jesus served people. For his disciples, this was perhaps modeled most visibly on the night of his betrayal. When Jesus gathered them in the upper room for a final time to celebrate the covenant meal together, he rose from the table, knelt before them with the towel and the basin, and washed their feet (John 13:1–16). His act of humble service also included direct instruction: "If I then, your Lord and Teacher, have washed your feet, you also ought to wash one another's feet. For I have given you an example, that you also should do just as I have done to you" (John 13:14–15). Jesus certainly practiced what he preached!

In fact, Jesus not only defined and modeled servant leadership but epitomized it. The greatest display of selfless and loving sacrifice was the willing surrender of his own innocent life for the sake of undeserving, guilty sinners. He characterized his substitutionary death as the ultimate act of service and the very reason he came, "to serve, and to give his life as a ransom for many" (Matt. 20:28). Similarly, Paul recognized Christ's sacrificial death as the greatest personification of service and as the greatest motivation for service. In his letter to the Philippians, he described Christ's incarnation, his "empt[ying of] himself, by taking the form of a servant," and his crucifixion, "death on a cross," as acts of humble service (Phil. 2:6–8). Paul's preceding instruction for believers—"Do nothing from selfish ambition or conceit, but in humility count others more significant than yourselves" and "look not only to [your] own interests, but also to the interests of others" (Phil. 2:3–4)—was rooted in the person and work of Christ. Thus, Christ's heart for serving others is both the example and the impetus for our service (Phil. 2:5).

Based on Jesus's life and ministry, it's impossible to construct a paradigm for expositional leadership apart from understanding it as servant leadership. This means that, practically speaking, we can't lead others without serving others. Typically, when we refer to servant leadership in ministry, we describe a willingness to perform menial tasks, an effort that elevates others and lessens ourselves, and a meek or deferential disposition. But in many ways, preaching requires exactly the opposite. Our sacred task is anything but menial. We are thrust to the forefront with a public platform where we can't be anonymous. And we're called to exhibit confidence and conviction that is bold and assertive.

So, how can we exercise servant leadership from the pulpit? Like any aspect of true preaching, it will be accomplished through our faithfulness to the sacred text. But beyond textual fidelity, servant leadership will ultimately be determined by the condition and disposition of our heart. Through the faithful exposition of God's word, we can honor the Master we serve, embody his character with the methods we employ, and reflect his heart in the motives we adopt. Each of these not only models what it means to be a servant but also displays the heart of Jesus, the ultimate servant-leader. As we attempt to translate these foundational principles into corresponding practices, there are several distinguishing marks that will establish our expositional leadership as servant leadership.

## Servant-Leaders Are Distinguished by Who They Serve

The servant's identity is always defined by the servant's master. Jesus frequently taught his disciples that as his servants, they would be identified by their association with him. As a result, they could expect insults, rejection, hatred, and persecution (Matt. 10:16–25). As Jesus explained it, "'A servant is not greater than his master.' If they persecuted me, they will also persecute you" (John 15:20). He also said, "Whoever receives you receives me" (Matt. 10:40) and "The one who rejects you rejects me" (Luke 10:16). Even though the servant can't determine how he will be received by others, he is responsible to clearly identify himself by the one he represents.

Jesus also taught his followers that they would be identified by their allegiance to him. The nature of the relationship between Christ and his disciples is characterized by the loyalty and obedience of servants to their masters. Jesus described this unrivaled devotion and its mutually exclusive nature when he declared, "No one can serve two masters, for either he will hate the one and love the other, or he will be devoted to the one and despise the other" (Matt. 6:24). Likewise, Paul described the allegiance of a servant based on his obedience to his respective master by posing the rhetorical question, "Do you not know that if you present yourselves to anyone as obedient slaves, you are slaves of the one whom you obey?" (Rom. 6:16). Simply stated, we're all a slave to someone or something, and our allegiance and obedience reveals the true identity of our masters.

According to Jesus, his servants would also be defined by the assignment he gave them. As he washed their feet and instructed them to do the same for others, he challenged them with the assertion that "a servant is not greater than his master, nor is a messenger greater than the one who sent him" (John 13:16). In other words, leaders wouldn't ask someone to do something they weren't willing to do themselves. But it goes beyond this and has greater implications for us as servants of our Master. The task given to the servant ultimately reflects the desire of the master for both—the servant who is appointed to the role and the specific task that is assigned.

Thus, servant leadership begins by recognizing our role as Christ's servants. Our association with him, our allegiance to him, and our assignment from him all position us to be recognized by our service to him. In practical terms, the foundational truth of our identity as his servants should put our ministry into its proper perspective. Like Paul, we must recognize that our place in God's kingdom is only the result of his undeserved kindness to us. The apostle described his ministry as that which he received "by the mercy of God" (2 Cor. 4:1). Paul recognized that he was unworthy to be used by God and yet, by his grace, God had chosen him and appointed him to his service (1 Tim. 1:12–14). This became the source of Paul's security and his sufficiency in ministry. He wrote, "Such is the confidence that we have through Christ toward God. Not that we are sufficient in ourselves to claim anything as coming from us, but our sufficiency is from God, who has made us sufficient to be ministers of a new covenant" (2 Cor. 3:4–6; cf. 1 Cor. 15:10). As a result, Paul's life and ministry were defined by his Master.

In the same way, we have been commissioned and commanded to serve our King. When we were adopted into his family, we were simultaneously appointed into his service. We have been deployed as servants of the King, and this distinguishes us in a couple of ways. Primarily, this means that we serve at the King's pleasure. Since we have received our ministry and calling from him, we are ultimately accountable to him. Therefore, we don't have the freedom to choose how, when, or where we serve. He gives us our assignment and we must determine that we will not be distracted, dissuaded, deterred, or discouraged from pursuing those things that delight, honor, and please him. We don't have permission to deviate from our duty as his servants.

Serving at the King's pleasure also means that he sets our agenda, determines our priorities, chooses our direction, and defines our role. And our servant's role is that of a spokesman who is duty bound to faithfully declare his word. We are his representatives who have been "commissioned by God" (2 Cor. 2:17) as "servants of Christ" and stewards of his truth (1 Cor. 4:1). We have been designated as "ambassadors for Christ" who speak on his behalf, operate under his authority, and deliver our King's message (2 Cor. 5:20).

Although we may pledge our loyalty to him, sometimes we can be tempted to betray our calling and begin to serve our own interests instead of the King's. When we face public scrutiny, congregational pressure, or personal opposition in our church, we can begin to preach from a place of self-preservation. But we must be mindful that when we find ourselves attempting to please people, we're no longer pleasing God (Gal. 1:10). On the other end of the ministry spectrum, when things are going well and our pride begins to swell, we can begin to preach for self-promotion. In doing so, we become showmen instead of spokesmen, preachers who love the applause of people more than the approval of the King (John 12:43).

As his servants, our security and confidence must be found in the identity of our Master. Our joy and contentment must be found in that which honors and pleases our King. Thus, when we faithfully expound his word and deliver his message, we can be satisfied with the fact that "we are unworthy servants; we have only done what was our duty" (Luke 17:10). He is the King, and it is an honor and privilege to serve at his pleasure.

In our role as servant-leaders, we not only serve at the King's pleasure but also serve the King's people. By God's grace, we have been entrusted with the role and responsibility to care for his church, to shepherd his sheep. Peter described our humbling leadership assignment and its corresponding approach when he challenged his fellow elders to "shepherd the flock of God that is among you, exercising oversight, . . . not domineering over those in your charge, but being examples to the flock" (1 Pet. 5:2–3). While all believers are called to "serve one another" in love (Gal. 5:13), pastors have an even greater responsibility to model the leadership of Jesus by serving others.

Too many times as leaders we operate as though the church exists to serve us when, in reality, it's the other way around. And while it may be easy to serve our people when they're being kind and supportive, our obligation to serve them doesn't change when our ministry becomes more challenging. In Corinth, Paul was mistreated and misunderstood by people he had invested in through multiple visits and an extended season of ministry. He had served them faithfully by "teaching the word of God among them" (Acts 18:11). But as Paul dealt with difficult people and circumstances in the Corinthian church, he didn't flex his leadership muscles or exert his positional authority as an apostle. He doubled down on his role as their "servant . . . for Jesus' sake" (2 Cor. 4:5). His disposition as a servant is what defined his leadership.

One of Paul's goals in 2 Corinthians was to differentiate himself from those who he sarcastically referred to as "super-apostles" (2 Cor. 11:5).

These were false teachers who were anything but servants. They had elevated themselves based on their impressive oratory skills, spiritual experiences, and imposing physical stature and status. So Paul distinguished himself from them by defending his integrity and describing several aspects of his servant-oriented ministry. In particular, Paul used his preaching as his primary evidence, and in doing so, he identified some important characteristics of servant leadership from the pulpit.

In the initial defense of his preaching ministry, Paul clarified his methods. As a servant-leader, the apostle knew that his ministry approach would be distinguished by the honesty and integrity that he exhibited. For this reason, he "renounced disgraceful and underhanded ways" (2 Cor. 4:2). He wanted nothing to do with secret and shameful practices or ministry shenanigans. While others adopted an underhanded approach, Paul distanced himself from back-hallway deals, sealed with a wink and a handshake, and ministries that served as a front for some selfish or dishonest enterprise. He also refused "to practice cunning" (2 Cor. 4:2), a term that was used to describe Satan's deception of Eve (2 Cor. 11:3). Paul would not allow his preaching ministry to be marked by sly and deceptive ways that sought to manipulate people to get what he wanted. He was not a spiritual con man, and as servant-leaders, we can't be either.

In the same passage, Paul also clarifies his message. He and other faithful leaders refused "to tamper with God's word" (2 Cor. 4:2). This quality would have been easy to assess by the public nature of his preaching and its coherence with the Scriptures. Paul would not, under any circumstances, dilute or distort God's word to make it more palatable. He was not an ear tickler (cf. 2 Tim. 4:3), an ego stroker, or a people pleaser. He was not a flatterer, and he certainly wasn't a false teacher.

In an effort to address the most important characteristic that validated his ministry, Paul also clarified his motives. As he laid out the evidence, he was willing to "commend [himself] to everyone's conscience in the sight of God" (2 Cor. 4:2). This open transparency implies that there was an undisputed integrity to his motives—he was trustworthy. His obedience to Christ and care for God's people were above reproach, without question, and obvious for everyone to see. He put it all out there. It's almost as if he welcomed their scrutiny and evaluation of him according to the biblical standards. This would have most certainly been in contrast to the others who were deceiving the church, those who were "peddlers of God's word" (2 Cor. 2:17). But notice that his ultimate accountability was "in the sight of God," the King he served. His motives were pure and focused exclusively on the kingdom.

In our own ministries, our leadership must be marked and measured by sincere hearts devoted to serving the King and leading his people. But evaluating the sincerity of our hearts requires asking some hard questions and receiving some honest answers. For instance, do you recognize the undeserved privilege that God has extended to you by inviting you to serve him and his people? Or do you serve with an entitled attitude that operates as though the King is fortunate to have you on his team? While we may not ever imagine expressing it that way, when we frequently complain about our ministry context or criticize those we're called to serve, it may be evidence of a proud and presumptuous heart. This soured spiritual condition can also be detected if we become unwilling to serve at the King's pleasure and are only willing to serve in ways that bring us pleasure. So, in your honest reflection, are you focused on and frustrated by your role, thinking that you deserve or are ready for more, or are you envious of others' roles and ambitious to advance? We can't be consumed with the role we have; rather, we must be consumed with the King we serve!

The loyal service we are called to offer our King is similar to how we might understand a combat soldier following an order from his superior officer. The officer's command is unquestioned; the soldier's obedience is unqualified. And while he operates in submission to his commander, his efforts ultimately serve the civilians he's defending. In essence, by serving one, he serves the other. Paul actually used this very illustration in instructing his young pastoral protégé, saying, "No solider gets entangled in civilian pursuits, since his aim is to please the one who enlisted him" (2 Tim. 2:4). Our duty is to please the King by serving his people. Thus, in order to effectively exercise servant-leadership from the pulpit, we should not be known for who we are—we must be distinguished by who we serve.

## Servant-Leaders Are Distinguished by How They Serve

In addition to being set apart by who they serve, servant-leaders will also be distinguished by how they serve. How they serve includes the type of actions they perform and the type of attitudes they exhibit. These practical expressions of servant leadership are the most visible indicators and the most tangible forms of what servant leadership looks like. And ultimately, they can determine one's effectiveness. It's similar to a waiter at a fine restaurant who brings you an exquisite meal. If his delivery lacks courtesy and kindness or is sloppy and indifferent, the quality of the food will be overshadowed by how he serves. For us as preachers, this means that it's not just the substance of our messages but also how we deliver them that ensures the spiritual food we serve is presented in a way that honors the chef and allows our patrons to savor the excellence of his work.

In order to serve and lead effectively from the pulpit, we must display a heart of love when we preach. The heart of a servant is made obvious by how he performs the task he is assigned. If it's done grudgingly or apathetically, it reveals a heart of disrespect toward the master he serves. If it's done with arrogance or aggression, it reveals a heart of superiority toward the people he serves. But, when his duty is performed carefully and thoughtfully, it displays a heart of sincere affection for his master and the people. In the same way, our preaching should reflect a heart of love for our Lord and his church.

The love a shepherd has for his sheep should be obvious in how he feeds them. This begins with our responsibility to evaluate their spiritual maturity and consider how to help them digest the weighty truth of God's word (Heb. 5:12–14). We must exhibit patience when they don't respond to our guidance by incorporating the Scriptures into their lives. We also can't take it personally when there's a lack of affirmation or appreciation for our preaching. In fact, we must be willing to receive criticism, even when it's unfounded, and our people must see that we are humble and teachable. Servants don't serve to be told, "Good job!" and they shouldn't get upset if someone shows them where they can improve. As servant-leaders, when we face these situations and responses to our preaching, we must exhibit patience and long-suffering by absorbing the heat and shining the light. As Paul writes in Galatians, "Let us not grow weary of doing good, for in due season we will reap, if we do not give up" (6:9).

Another way we exhibit servant leadership and display a heart of love in our preaching is through the even-handed treatment of our people. There's no room for preference or prejudice in the church (James 2:1–9). Although we're probably unaware of it, there are times in our preaching when we unintentionally do show partiality and make distinctions among our people. For instance, on Mother's Day we may overlook those who desire children but are unable to have them or those who may have recently lost their mother. While holidays like this one may occur infrequently, we often limit our weekly illustrations and applications to groups of people that are the most familiar to us or that fall into the typical church member category. Further, when we preach to the choir, we run the risk of marginalizing portions of our members. These aren't common ways we think about preferential treatment, but they certainly do ignore certain segments of the congregation while focusing on others. Though we can't consider every scenario or life circumstance represented in our hearers, we should strive to be mindful of everyone in a way that displays a heart of love as we lead and serve our people.

Perhaps the most obvious expression of love from the pulpit is reflected in how we address matters of sin. To be clear, we should never minimize sin or shy away from addressing cultural issues that are biblically immoral and unethical. But our tone must be loving and compassionate toward people who currently struggle with those things, made past decisions that they now regret, or have family members or close friends who are lost and living an ungodly lifestyle. We must guard our hearts from being critical of others or flippant about their struggles. No one should ever mistake our clearly stated biblical convictions for a lack of compassion. As Paul described his approach during his extended ministry in Ephesus, he "did not shrink from declaring . . . anything that was profitable" (Acts 20:20) and he "did not shrink from declaring . . . the whole counsel of God" (Acts 20:27). At the same time, he also did not cease to "admonish every one with tears" (Acts 20:31). In other words, while his preaching ministry was bold and uncompromising, he was also loving in his confrontation, caring in his correction, and sympathetic in his counsel.

Simply stated, there must be a warmth to our preaching and pulpit demeanor. As we confidently proclaim God's word, people should still see us as approachable and accessible. While we may think our boldness demonstrates a godly resolve, it often communicates an arrogant and aggressive disposition that is intimidating and seems insensitive. Christ, who characterized himself as "gentle and lowly" (Matt. 11:29), is not honored when his messengers are harsh and angry. We can be both courageous and compassionate. As we preach with passion and patience, our heart of love should be obvious. This servant-leader heart endears us to our people and compels them to follow our example (Phil. 4:9).

In addition to a heart of love, we must display a heart for the lost when we preach. One of the most influential aspects of our sermon delivery and demeanor is the example we set for our people in how we view and engage with those who don't know Jesus. Oftentimes, when we speak about unbelievers who have unbiblical values and viewpoints, we portray them as enemies who we must defeat and destroy instead of wounded victims who we must reach and rescue.

However, when the apostle Paul describes those who are lost, he does so in a way that demonstrates a genuine love for them. For example, he repeatedly references unbelievers who reject the message of the cross as "those who are perishing" (1 Cor. 1:18). Similarly, he described the gospel and his ministry as the aroma of death to "those who are perishing" (2 Cor. 2:15–16). He went on to explain that the hearts of "those who are perishing" are veiled, and they are blind to the gospel (2 Cor. 4:3). Overall, describing them this way would probably not be recognized or received as "loving" in Paul's context any more than it would in our culture. But the compassion displayed in this phrase reveals a heart of love in a couple of ways.

First, it demonstrates that Paul sees lost people through a spiritual lens. In other words, he sees them as image bearers who are spiritually dying and decaying, souls who are suffering, and people who are blind. Paul isn't seeing through the lens of hate or indifference—he is burdened for them in their unregenerate state. He recognizes that they are blinded by sin. The gospel is veiled to them and they're unable to see the truth of God's holiness, their own sinfulness, and Christ's forgiveness. Such sin is deceptive in that they are convinced they see things clearly, when in reality, they are indeed blind. But they cannot be convinced of this through our persuasion or arrive at this conclusion through their own reasoning. It's only when they turn to Christ that "the veil is removed" (2 Cor. 3:16). In addition to their sin, they're also blinded by Satan. The prince of the power of the air, the "god of this world," has "blinded the minds of the unbelievers, to keep them from seeing the light of the gospel" (2 Cor. 4:4). Our enemy is real and he is actively working as the deceiver to lead unbelievers to their destruction. God's word teaches us that Satan "disguises himself as an angel of light" (2 Cor. 11:14). Satan is the master manipulator; he is in the business of creating counterfeits. He himself is one. His "wicked deception for those who are perishing" is another reason why our hearts must break for them (2 Thess. 2:9–10).

Second, Paul sees the lost through an eternal lens. He recognizes that their current state of "perishing" will one day become an eternal state of death, separated from Christ for all of eternity, as they are literally being destroyed. This motivates him to preach with compassion, urgency, and desperation so that they might be rescued by the gospel. Although the world may hear this as a message of fear and punishment, it is actually a message of love. The gift of God's Son is an expression of his love, and personal faith in his atoning sacrifice guarantees that "whoever believes in him should not perish but have eternal life" (John 3:16). Though we are sinners who are perishing, God demonstrated his love through Christ's death for us (Rom. 5:8). John says, "In this is love, not that we have loved God but that he loved us and sent his Son to be the propitiation for our sins" (1 John 4:10). As one who had been captured by God's love, Paul was now compelled by the life-changing love of the gospel to show and share God's love with others. He had calibrated his heart to default to love and it was evident in his preaching.

Yet, despite the integrity of Paul's ministry, the purity of his motives, and the clarity of his message, he wasn't automatically welcomed or received by everyone. We must accept this same sobering reality. Paul understood that people would reject the gospel not because of his lack of clarity or compassion, but because of their spiritual condition. Because of this, their rejection didn't make him obstinate, argumentative, or combative. Instead, he displayed a heart of love that reflected our Master's, and this same love should be a distinguishing mark of our preaching ministry.

One thing Paul seemed keenly aware of was his own previous condition—being helpless and hopeless apart from Christ. It's easy for us to lose sight of the fact that before our salvation, "we all once lived in the passions of our flesh, carrying out the desires of the body and the mind, and were by nature children of wrath, like the rest of mankind" (Eph. 2:3). Like the lost around us, "we ourselves were once foolish, disobedient, led astray, slaves to various passions and pleasures, passing our days in malice and envy, hated by others and hating one another" (Titus 3:3). But it was "because of the great love with which he loved us, even when we were dead in our trespasses" that he saved us by his grace (Eph. 2:4–5). It was "the goodness and loving kindness of God our Savior" that saved us (Titus 3:4–5). Having this perspective is crucial because it's only when we're mindful of our own desperate need for Christ and the undeserved salvation that we've received that we will be motivated to love the lost.

You may now be wondering, how is displaying a heart for the lost in our preaching a distinguishing mark of servant leadership? Actually, Paul saw it as essential in his efforts to reach the lost and to lead others to do the same. His spiritual burden and unrelenting passion to see others come to Christ is evident in his proclamation to the

Corinthians: "I have made myself a servant to all, that I might win more of them. . . . I do it all for the sake of the gospel" (1 Cor. 9:19, 23). As he explains, his efforts were "not seeking [his] own advantage, but that of many, that they may be saved" (1 Cor. 10:33). He then challenges the church, "Be imitators of me, as I am of Christ" (1 Cor. 11:1). Perhaps our servant leadership will never be more evident than when we are leading God's people to serve others by living on mission and sharing his love with "those who are perishing."

These aspects of servant leadership also require us to evaluate our hearts by asking some introspective questions. For example, do you serve others with a heart of love and a heart for the lost or are you largely indifferent to their condition? Does your apparent indifference derive from a failure to appreciate your own previous blindness or is it simply a disgust for sinners that fails to recognize their inherent and eternal value? Perhaps the most penetrating questions are those that are the most practical. Are you angered and annoyed by those that don't know Jesus more than you are concerned and compassionate toward them? In other words, is your heart bothered by the lost or burdened for the lost?

While these questions may seem direct, it's crucial for us to honestly evaluate our hearts in order to rightly assess our servant leadership from the pulpit. Sadly, Christians have become known more for what we're against than what we're for in our culture. This can be especially true for us as pastors. We can easily become known more for our heat than our heart. But in the same way that peacocks have feathers, leopards have spots, and tigers have stripes, we should be distinguished by our hearts of love and our hearts for the lost as we faithfully preach God's word and exhibit servant leadership.

## Servant-Leaders Are Distinguished by What They Serve

These days it's not uncommon for leaders to overpromise and under-deliver. When those in positions of influence make guarantees and don't follow through, it's typically referred to as "lip service." Israel's leaders in the Old Testament were guilty of this, and Jesus indicted the religious leaders of his day as hypocrites for doing the very same thing:

"This people honors me with their lips, but their heart is far from me" (Matt. 15:8; cf. Isa. 29:13). But notice, their hypocrisy was not simply saying one thing and doing another. Rather, they also touted themselves as God's spokesmen but replaced his message with their own. Jesus thus chastised them, "For the sake of your tradition you have made void the word of God . . . teaching as doctrines the commandments of men" (Matt. 15:6, 9). They were spiritual frauds who were guilty of perpetrating a bait and switch. And if we're not careful, we can become guilty of the same thing when it comes to our ministries. As heralds of the King, our service and our leadership will be measured by *what* we serve—the message we deliver.

Overall, true service is always evidenced by the corresponding actions it performs. Jesus didn't just describe himself as a servant but actually followed through by serving others. He traveled great lengths and went out of his way to minister to those in need. He prayed over the bread and fish and distributed the multiplied portions to thousands of hungry people. He took the towel and the basin and washed his disciples' feet. He laid down his life for his friends *and* his enemies, carried the weight of sin on his shoulders, and endured our punishment by dying on the cross.

When it comes to preaching, our service will also be measured by its substance. In the same way that Jesus served, we must meet people at their point of need, break the bread of life for their spiritual nourishment, kneel in a posture of humility to address the ugly realities of their lives, and point them to the cross of Jesus as their only source of hope and salvation. This is how we serve God's people from the pulpit and lead them to deeper faith and trust in him.

In order to exert this type of servant leadership, we are called to deliver God's word. As we've discussed in previous chapters, the nature of Scripture and our role as God's spokesmen means that the biblical text must be the source and substance of our messages. But our role as servants also requires textual exposition because it provides the only remedy to meet people's needs. This doesn't mean that we're advocating for preaching to felt needs in a way that compromises the truth of Scripture for the sake of relevance or emotional support. It simply approaches the sacred task with an awareness that we are preaching to broken people who live in a broken world and need a loving Savior to heal their wounds, strengthen their weaknesses, and free them from the guilt and shame of sin.

As we lead our people with a servant's heart, our commitment to preach God's word allows it to accomplish its intended purposes. The Bible uses a variety of metaphors to describe itself, its life-changing purposes, and the effect it has when we faithfully proclaim it. Each of these scriptural images provides greater insight into how our preaching serves our hearers and meets their needs. For example, our preaching must scatter the spiritual "seed" that converts lost souls and gives new life through "the living and abiding word of God" (1 Pet. 1:23; cf. Luke 8:11). We must bring the spiritual "fire" and wield the spiritual "hammer" that melts and breaks the hardest of hearts that is full of pride (Jer. 23:29). When we faithfully preach the sacred text, we are also sending spiritual "rain" into the lives of our people that has the power to refresh their souls and yield spiritual fruit (Isa. 55:10–11).

Serving our people through the ministry of the word is also pictured as holding up a spiritual "mirror" that reveals their sinful imperfections and provides the healing remedy (James 1:22–25). Further, the "living and active" word of God will penetrate to the depths of our people's souls and dissect their spiritual condition by "discerning the thoughts and intentions of the heart" (Heb. 4:12). This work of conviction and correction is essential for their progress in sanctification. In addition, serving them the "pure spiritual milk" of God's word provides the spiritual nutrients necessary for their personal growth (1 Pet. 2:2). Faithfully preaching "the word of righteousness" helps them to "mature" by providing them healthy portions of "solid food" that satisfies their spiritual hunger, develops their spiritual discernment, and trains them to live in obedience (Heb. 5:12–14).

When our people are lost and looking for guidance, textual exposition will serve as "a lamp" for their feet and "a light" for their path (Ps. 119:105). As they fight their spiritual battles, our preaching equips them with the "sword of the Spirit, which is the word of God" (Eph. 6:17). And, when we serve them by expounding Scripture, we are dispensing eternal riches that are more valuable than gold, "even much fine gold," and satisfying them with savory morsels that are "sweeter also than honey and drippings of the honeycomb" (Ps. 19:10). Overall, the nature of our servant leadership must be distinguished by our faithful delivery of God's word. The divine nature of Scripture and its supernatural effects will meet our congregation's greatest needs, and through faithful exposition we can present timeless truths through timely messages that minister to God's people as we faithfully serve and lead them.

It's also important to recognize that the transforming power of Scripture will be personally experienced by our listeners through the life-changing truth of the gospel. This means that as we serve God in delivering his word, we are called to deliver good news. This reality should affect both the tone and the telos of our preaching. As fervent as we should be in declaring the truth, it's still good news. As faithful as we need to be in preaching justice and judgment, it's still good news. As direct as we may need to be in identifying and addressing sin, it's still good news. As honest as we must be in confronting cultural influences that may have crept into the church, it's still good news. As difficult as it may be to address hurting people in hard circumstances, we are still delivering good news.

The effectiveness of our servant leadership from the pulpit will be directly related to the level of gospel saturation in our preaching. As we highlight the redemptive truths of every preaching passage and apply the text through faith in the completed work of Christ, people will recognize our sermons as sincere efforts to serve them. Our preaching will be characterized by the truth, "How beautiful are the feet of those who preach the good news!" (Rom. 10:15; Isa. 52:7). The gospel will satisfy their souls and quench their spiritual thirst: "Like cold water to a thirsty soul, so is good news from a far country" (Prov. 25:25).

Overall, directing the hearts of our congregants toward the gospel will not only be our greatest act of service but also our greatest form of leadership. The apostle Paul makes the declaration for all of us as preachers when he says, "For what we proclaim is not ourselves, but Jesus Christ as Lord, with ourselves as your servants for Jesus' sake" (2 Cor. 4:5). In a culture and a context that was all about personal notoriety, Paul made it clear that his ministry and mission were all about serving others by preaching the gospel. He clearly recognized that the gospel was not about him, and he explicitly stated as much: "we [preach] not ourselves." Thus, as true servant-leaders, our declaration of the gospel is not meant to draw attention to ourselves, to gain followers, to impress others, to entertain, to promote an agenda, to spotlight our giftedness, or to stand on our favorite soapboxes. We are not some kind of hero to be celebrated. Rather, we declare the gospel to point people to Jesus.

Too many times in the church, we have elevated celebrity pastors, preachers, leaders, teachers, writers, and speakers. We have created a culture that looks to platform those with magnetic personalities, those who are gifted, and those who have a hip persona. In 1 Corinthians, Paul cautioned the church against this temptation when he heard they were debating whether they were of Paul or Apollos or Peter (1 Cor. 1:12). Sadly, living in the midst of the me generation and the age of social media, preachers are often found promoting themselves rather than promoting Jesus. We must be honest and ask ourselves, Are we more concerned with how many people know who we are or how many people know who Jesus is? Paul wanted nothing to do with a self-centered mentality; he wanted everything he did to be from a Christ-centered mindset. He didn't want to do anything that would interfere with or distract people from the gospel. He viewed himself as one who was at their disposal, simply there to deliver what they needed most, the gospel of Jesus Christ. If he fancied himself as anything, it was as a slave to Christ and a slave to others (2 Cor. 4:5; 1 Cor. 9:19).

So, what did he preach? The phrase used in 2 Corinthians 4:5 has been described by some as the gospel in shorthand: "we proclaim . . . Jesus Christ as Lord" (cf. Rom. 10:9–10; Phil. 2:9–11; 1 Cor. 12:3). Simply stated, he is "Jesus," the Savior of the world; he is the "Christ," the crucified Messiah, and as a result, he is the risen and reigning "Lord." Our submission and surrender to him, by faith and repentance, grants us freedom and forgiveness in him. This is the good news we proclaim. Our preaching ministry and leadership should be defined by this truth—we are "servants for Jesus' sake" (2 Cor. 4:5). We give our lives for the sake of others that the gospel may go forward. As servant-leaders we should be distinguished by what we serve, delivering God's word and the good news through faithful exposition of the biblical text.

## Conclusion

Being a servant isn't easy. It's often messy, it always requires personal sacrifice, and it typically goes unappreciated. In many ways, being a ministry leader is difficult for the same reasons. This means that we can expect the challenges that we face in our combined role as a servant-leader to be twice as hard. As a result, when it comes to our preaching, we can be less inclined to adopt a servant leadership approach because it may be the one place in our ministry that we feel like we can exercise unquestioned authority. But, in reality, our exposition of the Scriptures may be the most important place where our servant leadership is displayed. When done well, it will translate into more effective leadership in other aspects of our ministries. More importantly, it will enhance our preaching, translate into greater life change among our people, and honor the ultimate servant-leader, Jesus himself.

Our Savior's ministry exemplified what servant leadership looks like. While this is commonly recognized when it comes to his public ministry, it's also especially clear in his preaching ministry. As he proclaimed God's word as a servant-leader, he was distinguished by *who* he served. Jesus explained, "I have come down from heaven, not to do my own will but the will of him who sent me" (John 6:38). In particular, he spoke and taught according to what he heard from the Father and declared, "I always do the things that are pleasing to him" (John 8:29). In the same way, we embody servant leadership and faithfully represent the master we serve when we preach for the King's people according to the King's pleasure.

Jesus also distinguished himself as a servant-leader based on how he served in his preaching ministry. The gospels capture the heart Jesus displayed in his itinerant ministry: "Jesus went throughout all the cities and villages, teaching in their synagogues and proclaiming the gospel of the kingdom and healing every disease and every affliction. When he saw the crowds, he had compassion for them, because they were harassed and helpless, like sheep without a shepherd" (Matt. 9:35–36). Jesus's loving concern recognized the people's need for the spiritual guidance and sustenance that shepherds are intended to provide. Perhaps the absence of faithful preachers became even more apparent in contrast to his compassionate preaching of God's word and the people's desperate thirst for it. Thus, to be like Jesus, we must distinguish our exposition as servant leadership by how we serve when we display a heart of love and a heart for the lost.

Finally, Jesus distinguished himself as a servant-leader by what he served. The nature of Jesus's earthly ministry began with preaching (Matt. 4:17). The substance of his message was "the gospel" (Mark 1:14) and "the word" (Mark 2:2). Early on in his ministry, Jesus made it clear that he did not come "to abolish the Law or the prophets but to fulfill them" (Matt. 5:17). After his death, burial, and resurrection, he confirmed this reality: "beginning with Moses and all the Prophets, he interpreted to them in all the Scriptures the things concerning himself" (Luke 24:27). As the living Word of God, Jesus faithfully expounded the written word of God and "with many other exhortations he preached good news to the people" (Luke 3:18). All in all, our preaching should be characterized by the same attributes. We're called to distinguish our servant leadership through biblical exposition that faithfully delivers God's word and the good news of salvation that's available in Christ.

May we steward our responsibilities well, knowing that in the end, God will not commend us as preachers, pastors, or leaders, but as "good and faithful servants" (Matt. 25:21, 23).

# 5

# Situational Leadership from the Pulpit

*I will give you shepherds after my own heart,*
*who will feed you with knowledge and understanding.*

JEREMIAH 3:15

IT'S INTERESTING HOW PEOPLE describe unforeseen situations that arise in life. The Apollo 13 astronauts announced their crisis to the NASA Mission Control team in 1970 with some version of "Houston, we've had a problem" when an explosion disabled their spacecraft.[1] Since that time, many of us have used that same declaration to articulate our awareness of some challenging circumstance that we didn't anticipate. "I didn't see that coming!" and "We have a situation here!" are other ways people say that something has gone wrong and needs to be addressed.

Local churches are not immune to difficult seasons of trial, challenge, and hardship that they need help fixing. It may be in the form of a tragedy in the community, a conflict in the church, or a crisis in the nation or the world. And it's in those times that pastors have some of the greatest opportunities to shepherd people through their preaching. When our people are confused, afraid, disillusioned, or discouraged, they are longing for a word from the mountain. They need to hear some truth from God that will lash their hope to a solid mooring. As

---

1 "50 Years Ago: Houston, We've Had a Problem," NASA, April 13, 2020, https://www.nasa.gov/.

pastors, we must help them process unforeseen situations through a biblical lens and help them know how to respond in accordance with the gospel, shepherding them before, during, and after such situations by faithfully expounding God's word.

### Shepherding before Difficult Situations Start

The most important way to shepherd your people well during unexpected situations is to avoid waiting until crises arise. Pastors shouldn't wait for difficulty to surface before they determine whether or how to address it. This is because we can't always prevent the most undesirable situations from happening, but we can prepare our people to be ready for them when they come by sharing wisdom and knowledge they will need. Consider some ways you can prepare your people through preaching.

*Gospel Disposition*

One of the greatest gifts a pastor can give his people is the ability to think rightly about life, including crisis situations. What we're talking about here is the development of a Christian, or gospel, worldview. Pastors provide situational leadership in preaching when they intentionally preach to help their people view all of life through the lens of the gospel. If we had to choose between preaching to change the way people act and preaching to change the way people think, we should choose to preach to change the way people think. Why? Think of the old proverb that says, "Give a man a fish, you feed him for a day; teach a man to fish, you feed him for a lifetime."[2] When we give people a list of dos and don'ts to guide their behavior, they are often only helpful for an immediate, short-term, specific, and limited situation. But when we teach them to think through the lens of the gospel, we help them navigate every situation of every day of their lives. Our sermons can help our people develop a biblical worldview in several ways if we follow two instructions.

---

2    See Anne Isabella Ritchie, *Mrs. Dymond* (London: Smith, Elder, and Co., 1885), 342.

First, preach the gospel. The best way to teach the gospel is to preach the gospel. Don't assume your people know the gospel and can articulate it simply because they're members of an evangelical church. Greg Gilbert laments that the "gospel is surrounded by a fog of confusion."[3] "Ask any hundred self-professed evangelical Christians what the good news of Jesus is," he contends, "and you're likely to get about sixty different answers."[4] To overcome this ambiguity, we should, at the very least, highlight the gospel in every text that is preached because Christ is the theme of all of Scripture. Also, you might consider periodically preaching a doctrinal message or series on the tenets of the gospel and testing your people to make sure they know it and can articulate it. For example, you may periodically call for oral congregational responses to questions about the gospel, send out links to online surveys or quizzes, or offer training opportunities in having gospel conversations.

Second, appeal to the gospel. As you preach the gospel, look for specific life situations relevant to your people's lives that they need to consider through a gospel lens and appeal to the gospel as the criteria through which they interpret and navigate life. The apostolic writers frequently compelled Christians to look at everyday life through the lens of the gospel. They addressed practical issues like how to handle our money (2 Cor. 8:9), how to respond when we've been wronged (Eph. 4:32), how to relate to our spouses, parents, and employers (Eph. 5:22–27; 6:1, 5–9), how to live in unity by exercising humility (Phil. 2:5–8), and how to view suffering (1 Pet. 2:21–25). Surely, you will be able to find some way the gospel informs every part of the believer's life.

In addition to issues addressed in Scripture that are relevant for all believers, look for other issues that might be relevant for your people in specific situations. For example, how does the gospel inform the way believers should respond to public health guidelines, how the church should approach social justice, how Christian students should navigate dating, or how senior believers should spend their retirement? These

---

3   Greg Gilbert, *What Is the Gospel?* (Wheaton, IL: Crossway, 2010), 20.

4   Gilbert, *What Is the Gospel?*, 18.

and similar issues don't have to be the major thrust of the sermon if they're not the major thrust of the text, but they can be points of illustration and application. Everything in the believer's life should be interpreted and approached through a gospel lens, and pastors must help them do it through their preaching.

Third, finish with the gospel. Most of our sermons as pastors aren't likely to have a primarily evangelistic thrust for a couple of reasons. One is that most of the Bible was written to people who were assumed to be part of the community of God. Another is that true churches—by nature and definition—are comprised of regenerate people. However, in each gathering of God's people, there will probably be some unbelievers present (e.g., 1 Cor. 14:23–25). That reality should compel every pastor to make sure he shares the gospel and pleads with the lost to respond every time he preaches. While that sometimes may happen earlier in the sermon, pastors should make it a habit to never conclude a message without some kind of gospel presentation. Such a feature not only gives unbelievers an opportunity to be saved but also reinforces the gospel in the hearts and minds of the believers who are present.

### Doctrinal Comprehension

If the gospel is the story of the entire Bible, then a gospel disposition is one that is informed by the great doctrines of our faith that permeate the Scriptures. Right acting always follows right thinking, and right thinking is always determined by right doctrine. So, developing strong doctrinal convictions is an important partner in developing a gospel disposition. When Peter wrote "I will make every effort so that after my departure you may be able at any time to recall these things" (2 Pet. 1:15), he was stating his resolve to prepare believers with an arsenal of gospel truth they could draw from when circumstances arose that challenged their faith. Thus, pastoral preachers must strategically lead their people to know Bible doctrine so they can approach every aspect of their lives accordingly, including situations that they didn't see coming.

Not only does a working knowledge of Bible doctrine equip our people to interpret and navigate life through the gospel, it also postures them to be defenders of the faith amid the undermining of Christianity in our culture. Jude said, "Beloved, although I was very eager to write to you about our common salvation, I found it necessary to write appealing to you to contend for the faith that was once for all delivered to the saints" (Jude 3). In a world spinning out of control because of the effects of sin, Christ's disciples will find themselves more and more in situations that assault their Christian faith and challenge their biblical convictions. Thus, pastors must appeal to their people to contend for the faith that has been entrusted to them.

Whether it's unexpected situations that both believers and unbelievers face or situations in which believers find their faith under attack, life is filled with events and occurrences that God's children need to be prepared to navigate with Christian doctrine. Pastors can be intentional about teaching our people doctrine in several ways.

First, call attention to the great doctrines of the faith as they surface in your week by week systematic exposition. You don't have to abandon your current preaching plan to teach doctrine. Just look at the theological purpose of the passage you're studying and identify the doctrinal tenets that inform it or are informed by it. Doctrinal elements may not always be the main feature of the text, but you can still call attention to their presence and importance for your people.

Second, periodically preach a message or a series of messages from texts whose primary focus is one of the great doctrines of the faith. You don't have to abandon expositional preaching in order to teach on specific doctrines. Just find a biblical text that focuses on addressing one of the great doctrines of the faith. For example, you might preach a series on the doctrine of suffering from Romans 8, the doctrine of Christian stewardship from 2 Corinthians 8–9, or the doctrine of Scripture from Psalm 19. As you expound each passage, you can use other key texts that address that same doctrine as supporting material.

Third, periodically preach the great doctrines of the faith topically (or systematically), supporting each point from multiple places in the Bible. We've all heard one Bible expositor's caution about topical preaching: "Preach a topical sermon only once every five years—and then immediately repent!"[5] While we share this concern and affirm the need for cautiousness, doctrinal preaching will sometimes be a needed exception to the rule. Just like we've all been helped by good systematic and biblical theologies, our people can be helped by a good topical message every so often on a Bible doctrine that helps them see the whole of Scripture on the subject.[6] Tracing specific doctrinal themes through Scripture like covenant, redemption, and re-creation can make significant contributions to our people's arsenal of theological weaponry.

*Missional Determination*

Every believer in Jesus Christ has been left on the planet for the same purpose, and that is to "go . . . and make disciples of all nations, baptizing them in the name of the Father and of the Son and of the Holy Spirit, teaching them to observe all that [Christ has] commanded" (Matt. 28:19–20). Regardless of our individual career paths or spiritual giftedness, we all have this same life purpose. Regardless of the numerous ways we put food on our tables, we all have the same job description. Regardless of our respective local church mission or vision statements, we have all been assigned to this primary mission. And it's this mission that everything in our lives and ministries must be leveraged for.

With such a clear and specific task before Christ's disciples, every situation in life—expected or unexpected—should be embraced in view of this mission. Every believer must determine to approach all of life through the lens of the Great Commission. That includes challenging, unexpected, and even crisis situations like the one the apostle Paul found himself in at a Philippian jail. From prison, he wrote,

5   Walter Kaiser, *Toward an Exegetical Theology: Biblical Exegesis for Preaching and Teaching* (Grand Rapids, MI: Baker, 2006), 19.

6   Jim Shaddix, "Never Without a Word: Planning to Preach God's Revelation," in Jerry Vines and Jim Shaddix, *Progress in the Pulpit: How to Grow in Your Preaching* (Chicago: Moody, 2017), 52–53.

I want you to know, brothers, that what has happened to me has really served to advance the gospel, so that it has become known throughout the whole imperial guard and to all the rest that my imprisonment is for Christ. And most of the brothers, having become confident in the Lord by my imprisonment, are much more bold to speak the word without fear. (Phil. 1:12–14)

Every expected and unexpected situation should be seen by Christians as either roadblocks to or opportunities for gospel advancement. Having this perspective is simply another aspect of developing and living with a Christian worldview. And pastors should seize every opportunity in the preaching ministry to shape such a gospel mission mindset in their people. Here are some ways you can build missional determination in the members of your church through the preaching ministry.

First, teach your people about the grand missional emphasis of the Bible. If the gospel is the grand story of the Bible, then the gospel mission is its complementary narrative. Woven throughout the pages of Scripture from Genesis to Revelation is the Great Commission thread. In the Old Testament, God chooses Abraham to leave his homeland and go to a place where he would father a nation who would receive his blessing and be a blessing to all the people of the earth (Gen. 12:1–3). The psalmist prays that the nations would be made glad when God's salvation and power are made known throughout the earth (Ps. 67). Joel prophesies that God will pour out his Spirit on his children so they can prophesy about him (Joel 2:28–29). And God sends Jonah to Nineveh to call the people to repentance and announce his salvation (Jonah 1:1–2; 3:1–5).

In the New Testament, each of the four Gospels and the book of Acts record Jesus commissioning his disciples to take the gospel to the ends of the earth (Matt. 28:18–20; Mark 16:14–16; Luke 24:44–49; John 20:19–23; Acts 1:8). When the church is born on Pentecost, Peter declares the fulfillment of Joel's prophecy that God's children would testify about him (Acts 2). The Holy Spirit compels the church at Antioch to send missionaries to the nations (Acts 13:1–3). The apostle

Paul reiterates to the Romans his divine assignment to get the gospel to the Gentiles (Rom. 15). The two witnesses in Revelation represent the church's proclamation amid hostile pushback from the world (Rev. 11:1–13). And the Bible closes with the bride of Christ inviting all to come to him for salvation (Rev. 22:17)! These are just a few representative examples of the Bible's missional narrative believers need to be educated in so they can navigate every life situation as part of their life purpose, "always being prepared to make a defense to anyone who asks [them] for a reason for the hope that is in [them]" (1 Pet. 3:15).

Second, preach on a regular basis from great missional books and passages. In addition to some of the texts mentioned above, the Bible contains many passages that speak specifically to the believer's Great Commission responsibility. Consider developing a book series that focuses on the missional task of God's people from Bible books like Jonah in the Old Testament and Acts and Hebrews in the New Testament. Alternatively, you could preach standalone messages or theme-oriented series using texts like Matthew 9:35–38, Luke 9:51–10:12, and 2 Corinthians 5:11–21 to equip your congregation to always be mindful of their mission, even when life situations present themselves that don't necessarily seem connected to their evangelistic endeavors.

Third, look for the missional emphasis in every passage you preach. Similar to looking for doctrinal themes and relationships to Christ in every text you preach, always look carefully at your weekly preaching passage to see if it contains any elements related to the missional task, even if it's not a predominant theme. While you need to be careful to not perform hermeneutical gymnastics by forcing the Great Commission onto your text, the frequency of the missional theme in Scripture along with its dominant gospel emphasis mean there are many opportunities to highlight the mission of the church in your sermons. Take every opportunity you can in weekly preaching to feature God's mission and exhort your people to live intentionally on this mission in every circumstance.

Fourth, preach periodically on texts in which God's people overcome challenges to their mission. For example, Acts 6:1–7 is often shortsightedly interpreted as teaching on how to deal with conflict in the church, the need for shared ministry of the church, and even the historical foundation of deacon ministry in the church. However, a careful look at the narrative reveals that those elements are merely the immediate situational challenges to the church's mission of multiplying disciples, a theme that bookends the passage (Acts 6:1, 7). Look for passages in the Bible where believers face similar situations that threaten their ongoing gospel advancement efforts (e.g., Mark 1:35–39; Acts 3:1–4:31; 8:1–40; 2 Cor. 6:1–13; Phil. 1:12–18).

### Shepherding When Difficult Situations Surface

Sometimes a pastor's strategic leadership doesn't allow much time for strategizing. It's more spontaneous because life is often spontaneous. Thus, beyond the preparation we give our people in advance for navigating crisis situations, pastors must always be ready to lead their people when those kinds of situations actually emerge. These may come in the form of major events taking place locally, nationally, or globally that materialize without much warning. Overall, providing leadership in such times requires us to discern what God desires to say in the immediate season of crisis and then to boldly and compassionately declare that message to his people.

#### Divine Consultation

First and foremost among the pastor's leadership tasks when unexpected situations arise should always be consultation with the divine shepherd. We must go to God to access his wisdom and direction in shepherding his sheep. Consulting God really isn't a new theme in this book. We've already emphasized in chapter 2 the absolute necessity of preachers engaging the Holy Spirit in their ministries through prayer. And one of our underlying themes in every chapter is the call for our preaching to be driven by what God has said, which is the heart of exposition. The most strategic leadership pastors can give their people is to find out what God is saying, embrace it themselves, and expound it to others. But when situations arise in our congregation's life that nobody sees coming—crises that create discouragement and fear—the pastor's retreat to seek God's help is particularly urgent and important. There's no time that we need Jesus to be the "wisdom from God" (1 Cor. 1:30) for us more than when our people are in crisis.

God's people were in a crisis in Jeremiah's day. Judah's last righteous king, Josiah, had died and the nation had all but completely forsaken God and embraced rampant idolatry (Jer. 7:30–34; 16:10–13; 22:9; 32:29; 44:2–3). God's mercy had run out and his judgment was lurking on the horizon. King Nebuchadnezzar of Babylon would soon conquer and enslave the people of Judah (Jer. 24:1). This crisis left them in dire need of hearing God's voice, both his honest call for their repentance and his reassuring word of hope for their future. But instead of Judah's prophets rising to the task of pastoring God's people, they exchanged their shepherd's garb for sheep's clothing and became ravenous wolves among God's flock. And they also became the recipients of the scathing rebuke and condemnation of God (see Jer. 23:9–40).

What exactly were their offenses? For one, the Almighty chastised these shameful shepherds for not preaching repentance. He said "they strengthen the hands of evildoers, so that no one turns from his evil" (Jer. 23:14). He also reprimanded them for "filling [people] with vain hopes . . . visions of their own minds" (Jer. 23:16), telling people they were good to go and that no judgment would come their way (Jer. 23:17). God reproved them for preaching their own visions, for passing off their "dreams" as if they were his words, an unfaithful association that was as ludicrous as equating straw with wheat (Jer. 23:25–28, 32). Only his word wielded the consuming power of a fire and the crushing blow of a hammer (Jer. 23:29). God also castigated these prophets as the first plagiarizing preachers because they would "steal [his] words from one another" (Jer. 23:30). He even opposed them because they flippantly said "thus says the Lord" without first finding out what the Lord said (see Jer. 23:31)!

Numerous warnings for contemporary preachers grow out of the neglect of Judah's prophets in Jeremiah's day. Don't tickle people's ears by telling them what they want to hear. Don't be silent on the reality of God's judgment. Don't preach your own visions and dreams instead of his word. Don't plagiarize one another's sermons. Don't tell people that God said something that he never actually said. And there's certainly more. But one particular indictment looms over the rest—all the prophet's clerical crimes were rooted in one dominant dereliction of duty, namely, failing to be in the council of God. "If they had stood in my council," God said, "then they would have proclaimed my words to my people, and they would have turned them from their evil way, and from the evil of their deeds" (Jer. 23:22; cf. 18, 21, 28). Instead, they "lead my people astray by their lies and their recklessness, when I did not send them or charge them. So they do not profit this people at all, declares the Lord" (Jer. 23:32).

The supposed prophets of God had preached all kinds of sermons, but they had not heard and heralded what God said because they had not first gone to the source! They were intended to be God's mouthpieces, to vocalize to the people what he had revealed. Amid their crisis situation, his words were the only thing that could turn them away from their destructive evil and toward the righteous good that God desired for them. But although these prophets came to the people with a lot of rhetoric, they were bankrupt of any message of hope because they had failed to be in God's council. They brought the people no word from the mountain because they had not been there themselves.

Pastor, when crisis shows up at the doorstep of your church, don't run from it or ignore it. But at the same time, don't rush in and try to navigate it with your own know-how, wisdom, and experience. Your people need to hear from God, and they need to know that you've been with him in pursuit of his infinite wisdom. In the midst of crisis, people need to hear the truth, whether it be an uncomfortable call for repentance or an encouraging word of hope. And if you've consulted the Most High God, they will be more likely to receive whatever is needed in the moment. Before you go before your people with a sermon, get before God on your knees and consult the wonderful counselor. Pour over his word in order that you might hear his voice. Plead with him to give you wisdom to know where in his word you should take your people, what he wants you to say to them, and how he wants you to lead them. People can spot a man of God who's tarried in God's presence from a mile away. When you have been long with the Lord, your words and your direction will be a calming, soothing balm for your people in the midst of their turmoil. On the other hand, any attempt to exercise situational leadership from the pulpit without first seeking the face and voice of our omniscient and omnipotent God will prove futile, perhaps even dangerous.

## Prophetic Interpretation

Once we've been with God in the private place, our next responsibility is to interpret our contemporary situation through the lens of his counsel so we can speak prophetically to our people. Our steady diet of planned exposition and doctrinal instruction are vital, but those plans will periodically need to be put aside for God to speak in a timely way to an unexpected crisis or current event. Pastors will sometimes need to shepherd their people with a word from God that speaks to the immediate situation.

Prophetic interpretation especially needs to happen when things occur that end up consuming everyone's thinking. In other words, these are situations in which everybody is coming to church on Sunday with the same thing on their minds. It could be something like the public health crisis that affects the entire planet, a supreme court decision on an issue like abortion that affects a nation, a mass shooting in an elementary school that grips people across a region, or a recent decision that has divided a congregation. These kinds of unexpected events will periodically arise and consume the consciousness of an entire church. When they do, compassionate and discerning pastors shouldn't hesitate to interrupt their preaching calendars and allow God's word to speak prophetically and specifically to hurting and confused hearts.

When unanticipated events occur, people don't need to hear our empty efforts at trying to speak about something that we have no experience or expertise in. And they may not even need—at that specific time—to hear the next passage in our current expositional series. Rather, they need to hear the Almighty God speak prophetically into their lives with the infinite wisdom and healing balm that only he can give. While the expositor in us may want to plow through our planned series, the prophet in us needs to interpret the immediate crisis theologically and bring the people a word from the mountain.

To speak God's word prophetically into your people's immediate situation, follow the same path we discussed in chapter 3 for strategic leadership. Always begin by determining if God speaks directly in the Bible to the crisis or situation at hand. His people encountered famine and pestilence, rejection and persecution, opposition and war, disease and death, and a host of other challenges on their way to being shaped into his covenant community and fulfilling his mission. So, start by asking and answering the same question: Did God address this situation directly in the Bible? If he did, then the initial part of your prophetic work has been done. Just locate the appropriate text, interpret it in its context, develop your sermon on it, and challenge your people through faithful exposition of it, including careful application of its truths to their immediate contemporary situation.

If your contemporary situation isn't directly addressed in the Bible, however, then reorder your study process and employ the topical-theological-textual approach to Bible study and sermon development. In other words, start with your contemporary situation and then back up into the Bible. But only venture to do so with a clear rearview mirror that will allow you to find God's counsel with integrity. That begins with determining the theological implications underlying your situation. Ask probing questions like, How has human depravity created or influenced this situation? How can Christian people reflect the image of God in Christ in response to this situation? How can we seize this situation and turn it into an opportunity to advance the gospel? Think of more questions related to what the Bible teaches about God, humanity, and the gospel.

Once you've identified the theological issues that are related to your situation, identify a corresponding Bible passage that parallels one or more of your theological implications. Choose a passage that speaks directly to the doctrine or doctrines you've identified, one that makes significant contributions to the theological issues related to your situation. Once you've landed on a passage, exegete it objectively and interpret it according to your normal expositional process. As with strategic programming efforts, be sure not to allow your extra-biblical situation to unduly influence your interpretation of what the Holy Spirit inspired the text to say and mean. And don't forget to ground your interpretation in a main idea sentence about the passage.

With the right meaning of the text in hand, find the timeless principles to determine its relationship to people today. Remember that in some cases the significance of the text will be the same in modern times as it was in the biblical situation. But sometimes you'll need to convert it into a principle that's relevant for today. Once you've identified the principle in the passage, establish the connections with the contemporary situation you will be prophetically speaking into. Process the relationships between the principles of the text and your immediate situation. Determine how the theology of your passage is critical for your people to understand and navigate it in a fruitful and God-honoring way. Think through how the Holy Spirit's intent in the text speaks to your current situation. Identify how the passage's timeless truth is demonstrated in and through your situation.

Now you're ready to preach the Scripture's principle, making clear and careful application to the current situation you and your people have found yourselves in. Compassionately and confidently bring God's word—rightly interpreted and understood—to bear on the lives of the struggling people under your care. Remember, don't preach about your situation and attempt to retrofit the biblical text into it. Rather, preach God's intended meaning in the text and apply it to your situation with integrity. That's the only way you will speak a prophetic word into your people's lives, a word that originates in God's council. That's the only reliable and sufficient word that will enable them to hear his voice and successfully understand and traverse their journey through muddy waters.

## Shepherding after Difficult Situations Subside

The shepherd's leadership role is not over once crisis situations have subsided. Great opportunity and responsibility exist for pastors to both strengthen their people's faith and equip them to navigate difficult times in the future. In short, we can do this by regularly reminding our people about crises in the past so they will recall God's voice in similar situations in the future.

### People and Recalling

Just because people know something (or have even experienced it personally) doesn't always mean they will remember it in the future. Jude says, "Now I want to remind you, although you once fully knew it, that Jesus, who saved a people out of the land of Egypt, afterward destroyed those who did not believe" (Jude 5). How does that happen? How do people know something "fully" and yet not be able to recall it for future benefit? Well, it happens because of the fallen nature of these tents we dwell in, bodies and minds that are prone to forget. Even when we've heard God's voice and his counsel has helped us to navigate tumultuous waters, we have a propensity to forget his grace when similar situations arise in the future.

Case in point is Jude's reference to Jesus saving people out of Egypt and later destroying those who didn't believe. God delivered his children out of bondage and gave them his law at Mount Sinai (Ex. 20). But decades later, on the banks of the Jordan River, Moses had to preach an entire book's worth of sermons calling the people to remember God's law and not forget it when they possessed the promised land. The word "remember" is used fourteen times in Deuteronomy, and the word "forget" is used ten times. Moses knew the people's tendency would be to forget what they had learned and experienced. The rest of the Old Testament implies at least an assumption of the same bent. First and 2 Chronicles repeats many of the same stories that are told in 1 and 2 Samuel and 1 and 2 Kings. The psalmist repeats his acknowledgment of God's attributes and works over and over again, and the prophets rehash themes like law, judgment, and forgiveness in most of their writings.[7]

The New Testament isn't any different. The Holy Spirit wrote the story of the Gospel four times, and the first three were simply different viewpoints of many of the same stories of Jesus's life, work, and instruction. Even Jesus reiterated the truth by reusing some of the same sermons, parables, and object lessons. Maybe he did this because of different audiences, but maybe he also knew his listeners would be inclined to forget. The canon of Scripture itself seems to be a testimony to the help we all need in recalling important things.[8]

While God's mercies are new every day, his wisdom and faithfulness are reusable. He doesn't want his children to waste any of the lessons he's taught them or the experiences in which he's sustained them. He wants them to recall the steadfast love, faithfulness, and instruction that he gave them and apply it to situations they face in the future. But if we don't recall and revisit his grace from the past, we won't be able to use it when we later face similar challenges.

*Pastors and Reminding*

God's undershepherds are some of the main instruments he uses to help people recall demonstrations of his good grace. The ministry of reminding people of the difficult situations they've navigated with his help is an important part of the pastor's pulpit leadership. By helping our people remember both biblical and congregational history, we make a huge investment in enabling them to interpret and manage future history.

All in all, pastors have good biblical models for the ministry of reminding. In addition to the repetitive nature of the Bible noted above, two of the most important New Testament writers boldly embraced the role of reminder. The apostle Paul was unapologetic about repeating the same things. To the Romans he writes, "But on some points I have

---

7   Jim Shaddix, "2 Peter," in Jim Shaddix and Daniel L. Akin, *2 Peter and Jude*, Christ-Centered Exposition Commentary (Nashville: B&H, 2018), 20–21.

8   Shaddix, "2 Peter," 21.

written to you very boldly by way of reminder, because of the grace given me by God" (Rom. 15:15). To the Philippians he says, "To write the same things to you is no trouble to me and is safe for you" (Phil. 3:1). And he asks the Thessalonians, "Do you not remember that when I was still with you I told you these things?" (2 Thess. 2:5).

His apostolic associate Peter is no different. Peter actually assumes the reminding responsibility as his primary intent in his second epistle. In the face of his own impending death, he repeatedly takes up the memory motivation mantle at the very beginning of his letter, writing,

> Therefore I intend always to *remind* you of these qualities, though you know them and are established in the truth that you have. I think it right, as long as I am in this body, to stir you up by way of *reminder*, since I know that the putting off of my body will be soon, as our Lord Jesus Christ made clear to me. And I will make every effort so that after my departure you may be able at any time to *recall* these things. (2 Pet. 1:12–15)

Later in the book, Peter prods his people to recall the past again, saying, "This is now the second letter that I am writing to you, beloved. In both of them I am stirring up your sincere mind by way of *reminder*, that you should *remember* the predictions of the holy prophets and the commandment of the Lord and Savior through your apostles" (2 Pet. 3:1–2).

Pastor, in the days and months and years after a particular crisis situation subsides in the life of your congregation, remind your people of your prophetic words that guided them and of God's grace that sustained them. John MacArthur's explanation is needed for us: "All who preach and teach the Scriptures are reminding people of what God has said in His Word so constantly that His repetition and theirs makes truth stick."[9] In the end, reminding your people of their past will help prepare them for their future.

9   John F. MacArthur, *2 Peter and Jude*, MacArthur New Testament Commentary (Chicago: Moody, 2005), 49.

## Conclusion

Unexpected events, challenges, and crises are normal parts of church life because they're normal parts of life in general. Sometimes they're shared experiences with a community, a nation, or the entire world. Sometimes they're unique to all believers in Christ, and sometimes they're unique to a local congregation. Sometimes they're created by the normal circumstances of the human plight; sometimes they're the result of being associated with the person of Christ. Regardless of their nature or origin, situations often arise that create questions, confusion, discouragement, and even fear in the lives of Christian people.

When these situations do surface, they become the catalyst of one of two consequences in a local church. The congregants either handle them poorly and have their faith weakened, even shipwrecked, or they navigate them well and have their faith strengthened and matured. One of the main determinants of which one happens is the help the congregation gets or doesn't get from their pastor. If their pastor ignores or even downplays the situation, the sheep probably feel that God is silent and doesn't really care. If their pastor helps them hear God's voice clearly through his word—preparing them before crisis comes, speaking prophetically when it happens, and reflecting purposefully on it after it's over—their belief and confidence in God is strengthened and the church is matured. May God give us pastors who shepherd his people with courage and grace through the ministry of his word as they face the multicolored situations that characterize life during their sojourning in this world.

# 6

# Sensible Leadership from the Pulpit

*Avoid foolish controversies, genealogies, dissensions, and quarrels about the law, for they are unprofitable and worthless.*

TITUS 3:9

IF YOU'VE BEEN PREACHING any significant length of time, you know what shoe leather tastes like. What pastor hasn't stuck their foot in their mouth at some point in the pulpit? We've all had conversations lamenting these occasions and laughing at the various scenarios with other preachers as we recount our own mishaps. We may have even shared a video clip of one of these unenviable moments to ease our own humiliation!

To be fair, most of these moments are accidental and, in some ways, unavoidable (not to mention comical!). A mispronounced word or Freudian slip comes with the territory of our role as public speakers. Embarrassment and kindhearted ridicule are sure to follow, but the damage is typically limited to our egos (which can usually benefit from a slice of humble pie), and these mistakes rarely affect the church.

At other times, our offense, while still unintentional, is more significant and definitely not a laughing matter. To our own disgrace, we may inadvertently bring an untimely message that isn't mindful or aware of circumstances that people in our congregation are facing. What seems relatively innocent to us can reveal areas where we are tone deaf to the needs and sensitivities of others. These unintended wounds are regrettable, but most people are willing to accept a sincere apology when we acknowledge their hurt and express genuine remorse for our unawareness or insensitivity. Although they can be uncomfortable, these moments and conversations typically don't result in long-term harm or churchwide turmoil.

While people may be willing to look past our preaching potholes, we also must recognize the potential disruption and devastation that our pulpit leadership can cause. In working with young and aspiring pastors, as well as seasoned and scarred ones, the most frequent and tragic leadership failures we see are often the result of careless or reckless preaching. We're not talking about the kind that mishandles the text with sloppy exegesis or splits a church by espousing heresy, but the kind that abuses the pulpit, exploits the people, and elevates the preacher—this kind often brings the greatest harm.

Yet, these misuses are rarely the intended goal. Sometimes as preachers we can slide into unhealthy habits in response to situations in our churches or struggles in our own lives. We can be easily convinced to justify our approach by arguing that we're defending the truth, fighting the enemy, or boldly proclaiming the word. In reality we may actually be digging our heels in, taking a defensive and defiant posture, villainizing and bullying our people, or grandstanding under the guise of godly boldness.

Because these are often issues of the heart, the difference between such aspects of pulpit leadership can be impossible for our people to recognize. What's even more perilous is that they can also be difficult for us to distinguish. The difference between irresponsible leadership and sensible leadership is sometimes a fine line that's hard to discern. Thus, in order to identify and avoid these pitfalls in our own preaching, we must exercise sensible leadership that faithfully expounds the Scriptures, honorably serves our Lord, and responsibly cares for our congregations.

**Principles to Establish**

Sensible leadership is ultimately a matter of stewardship. It begins by recognizing the incredible privilege we have as those who occupy a sacred desk for a sacred task. When we operate from this conviction with unwavering resolve, it fortifies our commitment to preach God's word without polluting our messages with impure motives or diluting them with personal opinions.

Many of our leadership blunders in the pulpit result from a gradual drift away from the basic tenets that should anchor our preaching. When we are distracted by church dynamics, social and political issues, or personal ambition, we begin to filter our sermons through these funnels and compromise the integrity of the message and the pulpit. But when we maintain our biblical convictions about preaching and the pastor's role, it will properly orient our leadership toward the corporate implications of the text and help safeguard our sermons from misguided agendas.

The main tenet for sensible leadership in the pulpit is the weighty reality that we are stewards of God's truth. By definition, a steward's sole responsibility is to properly manage what has been entrusted to him. The servant who does this is commended as "good and faithful" for a job "well done" (Matt. 25:21, 23). The one who neglects his duty, even while giving the impression of being responsible, is condemned as a "worthless servant" (Matt. 25:30).

For the pastor, the primary treasure that has been entrusted to us is the gospel, and the primary task we have been charged with is to preach it faithfully. Paul described his privilege and obligation to "preach the gospel" as a "necessity" that constrained him, insisting, "Woe to me if I do not preach the gospel!" (1 Cor. 9:16). This assignment and corresponding conviction was derived from his understanding that as a preacher, he had been "entrusted with a stewardship" (1 Cor. 9:17; cf. Titus 1:3). Yet, this understanding was not unique to Paul's calling; it characterized the preaching ministry of the other church leaders as well. Paul described his ministry as well as Peter's as that of being "entrusted with the gospel" (Gal. 2:7).

In considering our own calling as pastors, our sacred stewardship must govern and guard our pulpits. In other words, this conviction should not only determine what we include in our messages but also what we exclude from them. We are required to "hold firm to the trustworthy word" (Titus 1:9) and avoid "swerving" from the truth by wandering "into vain discussion" (1 Tim. 1:6). Those who deviate from their charge "devote themselves" to ramblings that "promote speculations" rather than occupying themselves with "the stewardship from God" (1 Tim. 1:4) that focuses on "the gospel" they have been "entrusted" (1 Tim. 1:11) with. Instead, they must heed Paul's charge and plea to his young pastoral protégé: "O Timothy, guard the deposit entrusted to you" and "avoid the irreverent babble and contradictions" that cause people to swerve from the faith (1 Tim. 6:20–21).

As committed expositors, none of us would blatantly disregard God's word or irresponsibly exploit the pulpit. But, if we're being honest, we must confess that there have been times when we have taken an unauthorized detour in our messages to address an issue that isn't reflected in the text. We may attempt to justify these momentary excursions as pastoral privilege by loosely connecting them to the passage. But when we attach a thought or idea to the biblical text by including it in the sermon without an explicit explanation of how they relate to one another, we are implying that those issues and assertions carry the weight and authority of Scripture. At that point we have deviated off the path, misrepresented the Lord, and compromised our stewardship. This is homiletical treason. Ultimately, we are accountable, "not to please man, but to please God" as those who have been "entrusted with the gospel" (1 Thess. 2:4).

Taken to the extreme, it may sound like we're advocating for a strict approach to preaching that drowns the congregation in technical details or never mentions anything that's not explicitly referenced in the text. But holding firm to the word without swerving doesn't exclude sermonic elements like illustrations and applications, which are essential components of textual exposition. Sometimes the examples and implications of a biblical principle may be used appropriately to address relevant congregational, social, or political issues. We attempted to provide some practical guidance for these occasions in our treatment of strategic leadership in chapter 3 with these same convictions in mind. As faithful stewards of his truth, we must ensure that they are legitimate applications that derive from and are tethered to the preaching passage.

In addition to our stewardship of his truth, we must also remember that we are stewards of God's church. This reality defines what it means to be a pastor. It serves as the foundational truth that undergirds each of the required qualifications for the role as well as the overarching attribute for those who occupy the office. Paul writes that "an overseer, as God's steward, must be above reproach" (Titus 1:7). Therefore, it's critical for us to evaluate how our stewardship of God's people dictates and determines our leadership from the pulpit.

In the New Testament there are two primary images that depict the pastor's role and responsibilities as a steward. First, throughout the pastoral epistles, Paul pictures stewardship as managing a house. In his list of qualifications to Timothy, Paul draws an immediate parallel between the pastor's leadership of his family and his ability to lead God's people, writing, "He must manage his own household well . . . for if someone does not know how to manage his own household, how will he care for God's church?" (1 Tim. 3:4–5). He goes on to summarize his counsel to Timothy as that which is intended to provide guidance and instruction for "the household of God, which is the church of the living God" (1 Tim. 3:15). In keeping with this domestic theme, he also characterizes the intended interaction between church members in familial terms (1 Tim. 5:1–2) and describes their service within the church as vessels in God's house (2 Tim. 2:20–21).

In addition to using the illustration of a home, Paul also pictures stewardship as shepherding. As we mentioned in the first chapter, the most commonly used term for the office today, "pastor," actually derives from the biblical term for "shepherd." As overseers of "the flock," we are called "to care for the church of God" (Acts 20:28). The Lord has entrusted us as shepherds to care for his sheep as we operate under the oversight of the chief shepherd (1 Pet. 5:2–4). This means that we're called to serve at his pleasure, guide according to his direction, tend with his heart, and nourish with his word. Caring for the sheep must be our top priority. Therefore, our role and responsibility as preachers must consider their spiritual condition and operate according to their best interest.

As we saw in examining servant leadership from the pulpit, this doesn't mean that we tickle their itching ears, preach only to felt needs, or maintain peace at all costs. We will, in fact, have to address uncomfortable issues, confront sin, and call people to repentance. But as we do, we must be sure that "the aim of our charge is love that issues from a pure heart and a good conscience and a sincere faith" (1 Tim. 1:5). Our personal feelings and frustrations, dreams and desires, and opinions and objectives can't determine what or how we preach.

Ultimately, our stewardship of God's church is directly related to our faithfulness in the pulpit. This is because our role as stewards in leading God's people also involves our responsibility to steward our gifts well. As those who proclaim the Scriptures, we are called to use our spiritual gifts "as good stewards" and to preach "as one who speaks oracles of God" (1 Pet. 4:10–11). The pastoral office and calling are sacred, and as his messengers we are managers who can't violate our stewardship. We are accountable to God for how we lead his household and shepherd his flock, and we must order our preaching accordingly.

Overall, these two foundational convictions, that we are stewards of God's truth and his church, should serve as the gate or the guards that refuse to let unauthorized intrusions into our messages. As we prepare our sermons, we must be armed with these convictions and allow them to prevent the entry of personal opinions or agendas by inspecting the content of our messages to remove any contraband that is not faithful to the text. And in the end, we can trust the Lord to defend his territory and his spokesman, untangle the social and political knots, and change people's hearts through the power of his word.

## Pitfalls to Avoid

In seeking to be good stewards of God's truth and his church, we must also be mindful of the common pitfalls that can undermine our efforts to lead well. This begins by recognizing that sensible leadership from the pulpit is defined as much by what it avoids as what it includes. Practically speaking, this means that we must be diligent to avoid preaching landmines that can sabotage our ministry leadership and leave God's people dazed, confused, angry, or hurt. Sensible leadership recognizes how to identify and navigate these dangerous preaching hazards and avoid common contemporary pitfalls. Overall, there are three particular danger zones that we should make an intentional effort to evade.

One of the main ways we can exercise sensible leadership from the pulpit is to avoid public arguments. While this may seem obvious, it's actually one of the easiest and most common ways we detour into threatening territory in our preaching. Perhaps this is most apparent by how Paul continually addresses our propensity as pastors to be distracted from our primary role as preachers and cautions us against being lured into disagreements and disputes that we should avoid.

While repeatedly outlining for Timothy and Titus what to teach in the pastoral epistles, Paul also repeatedly outlines specific things to "stay away" from or "shun." Other than steering clear of certain types of people (2 Tim. 3:5), Timothy should also "avoid" things related to the content of his public instruction and personal interaction (1 Tim. 6:20; 2 Tim. 2:16; Titus 3:2, 9).

First, in both of his letters to Timothy, Paul specifically cautions him to "avoid irreverent babble" (1 Tim. 6:20; 2 Tim. 2:16). In our previous section regarding stewardship of the pulpit, we briefly mentioned his first admonition to avoid "pointless discussions" and "unholy chatter" in order to guard the truth of the gospel (1 Tim. 6:20). Interestingly, Paul's parallel warning in his second letter to Timothy immediately follows his command regarding diligence in studying and dedicating himself to "rightly handling the word of truth" (2 Tim. 2:15). The sequence directly contrasts his handling of God's word with the "irreverent babble" he's called to "avoid" (2 Tim. 2:16). Perhaps most significantly, he cautions Timothy that his failure to do so "will lead people into more and more ungodliness" (v. 16). In other words, avoiding these things and focusing on God's word determines the direction and effectiveness of a pastor's leadership from the pulpit.

Similarly, Paul's cautions Titus to "avoid quarreling" (Titus 3:2) and "foolish controversies" (Titus 3:9) because of the affect it has on those he leads and influences. The "quarrels" undermine our testimony as well as the gospel that our "courtesy" and kindness are meant to embody for those who are lost (Titus 3:2–7). God calls us to speak with great confidence about the gospel and its practical implications as we "insist on these things" that are "excellent and profitable for people" (Titus 3:8). By contrast, the "foolish controversies" and related disputes that we're called to "avoid" prove to be "unprofitable and worthless" (Titus 3:9).

So how does all this apply to our ministry today? Many preachers who desire to "contend for the faith" (Jude 3) and recognize our responsibility to "rebuke those who contradict" with sound doctrine (Titus 1:9) will adopt a defensive posture in the pulpit. While these are crucial aspects of our role, our preaching should not be characterized by an argumentative demeanor or confrontational rhetoric. And beyond our posture and tone, we must also be careful that our messages don't focus on unnecessary issues of debate and controversy.

Yet, engaging in public arguments doesn't always arise from an argumentative posture. As pastors, it's easy to get comfortable in the pulpit, especially when we've been with the same church family for an extended season. While familiarity lowers walls and opens doors for honest communication, it can easily become an opportunity for us to mishandle that trust and freedom by not filtering our words appropriately. We can begin to assume that our people will automatically understand what we meant to say, give us latitude to speak more freely, or give us the benefit of the doubt. But we must be careful not to use the pulpit to air grievances or pull out our favorite soapboxes. Taking these liberties and presuming on people's support can slowly and subtly start to erode our leadership.

Another important aspect of avoiding public arguments that requires an honest look in the mirror involves recognizing the sinful cravings of our hearts that feed on debates and controversies. Some people expect pastors to be the resident expert on many of the social issues in our culture. In an effort to satisfy these congregants and gratify our own desire for respect or notoriety, we can begin to relish our role as the neighborhood prophet who calls people out, turns heads, and raises eyebrows. We may not always do this with cultural issues but we can be tempted to do so with theological topics in order to pacify the same desires. Yet, as Paul charges Timothy, we should be reminded, "not to quarrel about words, which does no good, but only ruins the hearers" (2 Tim. 2:14).

In addition to avoiding public arguments, we must also be careful to avoid political agendas. These issues, specifically those that are not addressed by God in the Bible, are particularly dangerous because they are typically some of the most hotly debated, volatile, and potentially divisive ones. Political subjects can involve civil politics or church politics, but we must guard our messages from being motivated or controlled by either. To do so effectively requires wisdom, tact, and diplomacy. These attributes are not celebrated or conditioned in our culture, so they can be points of weakness for all of us. They also come more naturally to some and are typically acquired over time (by learning from our own mistakes!). But they are communication skills that can be developed, and they are essential for effective leadership, particularly when dealing with political issues.

When it comes to these sensitive topics, there are some foundational tenets that must shape our perspective and approach to politics in the pulpit. First, our identity is chiefly defined by who we are in Christ, not our ethnicity, gender, or political affiliation (2 Cor. 5:17; Gal. 3:28; Col. 3:11). Second, Scripture is the definitive authority on all issues of morality and ethics. This not only determines our positions on social and cultural issues but also informs our advocacy for rights, laws, candidates, and policies. And if civil statutes conflict with scriptural standards, we are not required to compromise our biblical convictions to comply with society's laws (Acts 5:29; 1 Pet. 4:14–16). Third, government authorities are established by God, and we are required to submit to them and support them accordingly (1 Pet. 2:13–14;

Rom. 13:1; Titus 3:1). While we must acknowledge that we do not live in a theocracy, we should celebrate and be thankful for our country, participate in our society as responsible citizens, and prioritize our ultimate citizenship in heaven (Phil. 3:20; Eph. 2:19). Fourth and finally, the church is Christ's body and bride, his chosen instrument to accomplish his redemptive plan on earth (Eph. 3:8–10). Therefore, any spiritual reform or revival that we seek will come through the faithfulness of God's people in reaching every nation with the gospel of Jesus Christ (Matt. 16:18; 28:18–20). While these tenets don't eliminate political disagreements among genuine Christians, they do establish the essential political truths that God's people can affirm. More specifically for us as preachers, they should undergird and restrict the political elements of our sermons.

It's interesting to note that Paul's letters to both Timothy and Titus address political issues. Yet, contrary to the typical approach in today's culture, his instruction to the young pastors never endorses slanderous behavior, much less combative or rebellious conduct, even though they lived in a politically hostile environment. Instead, Paul advocates for a posture of prayer that intercedes on behalf of government leaders and lives "a peaceful and quiet life, godly and dignified in every way" that serves as a testimony for the gospel (1 Tim. 2:1–5; Titus 3:1–7).

As we lead our people to embrace this biblical posture and perspective regarding political issues, we must model this ourselves in how we reference such issues in our preaching. Sometimes it's tempting to politically play to the crowd by making disparaging comments toward candidates, parties, or policies. Other times, we may convince ourselves that we've earned the right to speak freely, which becomes our license for unfiltered rants. But it's important to not unnecessarily offend members, guests, or even our communities with ill-advised and insensitive assertions or allegations. In the spirit of Paul's instructions, we should exhibit dignity and respect when addressing the related issues. But, most importantly, we should focus on our listeners' primary allegiance to Christ and his church and limit our political references to things that are relevant to the text.

This does not mean that we should shy away from giving guidance or speaking to moral, ethical, or civil issues at all. As God's spokesmen and stewards, we have a responsibility to help our people think biblically about crucial topics that have relevance for their lives. It not only informs their understanding but also equips them to engage in their social and professional circles with a scriptural perspective. When it's textually relevant we should address these issues with clarity and unwavering conviction in our messages. But we must be careful not to extend our comments beyond what the Scriptures say in a way that would inappropriately authorize what is essentially an opinion or a man-made principle. It's also important for us to distinguish between what should be included in our sermons and when we should look for other occasions and opportunities within the church to address these issues.

In addition to avoiding civil politics, we must also not use the pulpit as a platform to engage in church politics. Let's face it, when the political temperature in the church gets turned up, we feel the pressure to address certain situations or people from the platform. It may not be by directly calling someone out or addressing specific circumstances (although that temptation can be strong!), but we all know how to send a message while also maintaining a level of deniability. We can actually become quite good at this, and we may even convince ourselves that we're innocent of any intended insinuations. But the pulpit is not the place for political posturing that seeks to strong-arm church leadership, win people to our position, or undermine others' efforts or agendas. We must honor the sacred nature of the sermon and preserve its intended purpose.

Overall, when we are faithful to our task and the text, we can trust the Lord to fight our battles and our adversaries. And when we do, there will be times when the Spirit may convict someone apart from any intentional efforts from us to address a situation. As a result, the people involved may accuse us of some level of political maneuvering. While we certainly should not apologize for God's work, we should also be able to legitimately attribute their conviction to the Spirit because we have avoided subtle but deliberate jabs in our sermons, maintained our integrity, and responded with sincerity. Perhaps the most significant result of this is that the people who are unaware and uninvolved will be protected, and we will further establish our commitment to faithful exposition.

Though sensible leadership should always be mindful of our people, it also requires us to be self-aware and avoid personal ambition. This is a basic principle for all believers as we're called to adopt the mentality of our Savior (Phil. 2:3–5). But for pastors, not doing this is a particularly dangerous and common pitfall. In fact, in his list of qualifications, Paul warns Timothy of the proclivity of pastors to become "puffed up with conceit" and undermine their ministry and testimony (1 Tim. 3:6–7). This warning doesn't just confirm our own prideful inclinations, it cautions us to consider the alluring esteem of pastoral ministry, the intoxicating power of leadership, and the invigorating nature of preaching in front of people. These intrinsic perils of the pastoral office require us to frequently evaluate our motives, especially when it comes to preaching. Overall, the Scriptures identify several misguided or sinful ambitions that we must guard ourselves against as those who proclaim the gospel.

One of the main motivations that the Bible condemns for preachers is monetary gain. Paul distinguished "peddlers of God's word" from the nobility of faithful preachers as "men of sincerity" (2 Cor. 2:17) who proclaimed the truth with no "pretext for greed" (1 Thess. 2:5). He also forbade pastors from being "lover[s] of money" (1 Tim. 3:3) who shepherd the flock "for shameful gain" (1 Pet. 5:2). While most pastors do not enter the ministry for the financial benefits, the pressure to provide for our family, the sacrifices we feel responsible to make for the church, and the limited salary we often receive can cause financial gain to become a real factor. It can be difficult to untangle our sincere desire to care for our family and a selfish desire for financial well-being. While every ministry and family situation are different, we must prayerfully discern the motives of our hearts and never begin to view preaching as a means to an end.

Another selfish motivation we should guard our hearts against directly relates to our leadership. The power of influence may not be something we're initially thirsty for, but it can easily become something we begin to crave as we get a taste for it. Our responsibility to lead shifts from being a humble honor to a compulsive fix that feeds our ego and fuels our appetite for control and respect. When this happens, we will begin to manipulate and mislead people in order to accomplish our agendas by impressing them with our homiletical maneuvers. Our sermons eventually become gimmicks that handle the word of God like a prop to perform our spiritual stunts.

In his letters, Paul denounced this type of preaching and defended the integrity of his ministry based on the absence of such motives and methods. He argued, "Our appeal does not spring from error or impurity or any attempt to deceive . . . we speak, not to please man, but to please God who tests our hearts" (1 Thess. 2:3–4). Likewise, we must make sure that our preaching is ultimately for an audience of one—God himself. In our sermon preparation and delivery we must guard our hearts from the desire to impress others, to seek the empty praise of people, or to leverage the pulpit for personal influence.

One final aspect of selfish ambition that we must guard our hearts against is the desire for self-promotion. The public nature of preaching makes it a natural source for misplaced validation from the congregation that can easily lead to misguided aspirations in the heart of the preacher. Even though faithfulness should be our standard, we can quickly adopt a new metric of success that is measured in affirming comments, growing crowds, social media likes, and public recognition. When this shift happens, we can begin to prepare and preach our messages with the idolatrous goal of exalting ourselves instead of Christ. As a result, we become celebrities in our own minds and start to aspire to a larger ministry platform or more prominent church to feed our growing egos. This, in turn, sours us toward our current ministry context and fuels discontentment in our hearts. What began as a well-meaning desire to preach God's word quickly mushrooms into an all-consuming passion for status and recognition.

If our desires become intertwined with selfish intentions, it will eventually become obvious to our people and will compromise our leadership. A similar situation can happen in the home when God attempts to use our families to keep us humble, but we begin to view them as a thorn in our flesh. When we're blinded by selfish ambition in the pulpit, all the people we care about, from our immediate family to our church family, become pawns in our efforts to crown ourselves as a king. Sadly though, our desire for promotion and position ultimately results in our own ministry checkmate. As we seek to avoid selfish ambition, we must instead desire to make much of Christ.

### Precautions to Employ

Overcoming these common leadership pitfalls in the pulpit requires a strategy to combat them. The messy realities of pastoral ministry, combined with the sinful propensity of our hearts, should compel us to take a proactive approach. Such precautions will not only prevent unnecessary adversity but also serve as catalysts for faithful and effective leadership from the pulpit.

Like every aspect of our ministries, we must begin with honest reflection and an intentional effort to protect our hearts. In addition to recognizing sinful tendencies in our hearts that we are aware of, we must also recognize that we're capable of having "hidden faults" (Ps. 19:12). The deceptive nature of sin can keep us from seeing our struggles, and blind spots are the most common threats to sensible leadership.

To combat the sin that hides itself behind our biblical convictions and sincere intentions, we must pray strategically. We should start by celebrating the privilege of preaching as well as renewing our commitment as stewards of God's truth and his church. Frequently reminding ourselves of these sacred realities sharpens our focus and helps us to recognize competing motives that may be driving the interpretations, illustrations, and implications in our messages. Our prayers should also target several other deceptive and common enemies, including bitterness that we may be feeling toward church members; pride that may be driving certain agendas, powerplays, or an appetite for control;

and insecurities that may cause us to preach for compliments or self-promotion. Inviting the Lord to search and cleanse our hearts from these potential pitfalls is essential for maintaining sensible leadership.

In addition to protecting our hearts, sensible leadership also requires us to pray for wisdom. As we have seen with other aspects of our expositional leadership, prayer and divine wisdom are essential. It's no different with sensible leadership. So many of the issues we face in pastoral leadership have multiple dimensions that make them difficult to navigate. As we attempt to lead God's people from the pulpit, we need his wisdom to avoid the pitfalls that would undermine our ministry. Dealing with congregational tension, relational dynamics, political opinions, or social issues can be extremely complicated. We can struggle to know when to address certain situations, how direct to be, and whether such comments are even appropriate to connect to our preaching passage.

We also need God's wisdom to provide clarity and conviction that protects us from interpreting our passage through the lens of our context and circumstances. Additionally, we need his discernment to help us distinguish between the urgent and the trivial, public and private, preference and principle. God's wisdom further provides us with the terms, the timing, and the tone we need to address sensitive subjects from the pulpit. He graciously invites us to pray for wisdom with the assurance he'll provide it (James 1:5). While his Spirit guides us, we can also receive his wisdom through the counsel of other trusted leaders and fellow pastors. We can benefit greatly from their informed insights and their objective input, especially where our judgment may be clouded and our perspective may be limited. Through Spirit-led prayer, direction from his word, and guidance from others, we can rely on the Lord to give us wisdom as we exercise sensible leadership from the pulpit.

Once we have evaluated our own hearts and sought God's wisdom, we can then preach with confidence. Although this may not initially sound like a precaution, focusing on our sacred task and Scripture's authority liberates us from the pressures that often undermine our sensible leadership. Sometimes it's not our arrogance or agenda that compromises our leadership from the pulpit—it's our insecurities that make us second-guess our sermons, preach to appease people, or posture ourselves for favorable public perception. But when we preach the text and allow it to dictate our sermon content, we can preach with courage, trusting the Lord to honor his word and protect his messenger.

Our confidence also derives from the safeguard of an expositional approach that systematically preaches through extended portions of Scripture or books of the Bible. Planned sermon series that walk through sequential passages protect us from the accusation of manipulating our text selection to serve our own purposes. God's timing is providential, and when his word addresses a specific topic or situation, we can preach with humble confidence, knowing that we haven't put our hands on the wheel to steer things in a self-serving direction. As a result, we can focus on expounding the Scriptures and allow the Spirit to convict hearts and transform lives without worrying about how our messages will be perceived.

### Conclusion

We've all watched from a distance as other pastors fumble the leadership ball. In many ways it's heartbreaking because we can easily relate to the challenges and failures we've experienced in our own ministries. There's no sense of satisfaction in seeing a brother stumble. But it's also easy for us to Monday-morning quarterback the situation to identify how it could've or should've been handled differently and how the leadership collapse could've been avoided. While we certainly can learn from others' mistakes and pray against similar failures in our own life and ministry, the issues are much more difficult to recognize up close and in our own backyard.

This is why sensible leadership from the pulpit is so crucial. When we face the daily leadership challenges in our own ministries, they are compounded and quickly spiral out of control if we mishandle them from the pulpit. But, when leveraged properly, our preaching leadership can neutralize volatile situations in the church, combat the cultural issues in our world, provide spiritual guidance for God's people, and avoid sabotaging our ministry and pastoral influence.

Sensible leadership is grounded in the essential truths of God's infinite wisdom and the power of the preached word. These unchanging realities are also the basis for our stewardship as managers of God's house and shepherds of his sheep. As we navigate the various dynamics of expositional leadership, these convictions must serve as safeguards for the content of our sermons. Any temptation to leverage the pulpit beyond the textual limits of the preaching passage compromises the power of the Scriptures and our function as God's messenger.

While there are numerous pitfalls that can cause us to stumble in our stewardship, the three most common hazard areas that we must intentionally avoid are public arguments, political agendas, and personal ambition. Each of these threats target different aspects of our pride, points of personal and pastoral insecurity, and weaknesses caused by social and cultural pressures. But their power can be overcome by searching our hearts to identify spiritual blind spots, seeking godly wisdom through prayer and trusted counsel, and remaining faithful to the text as we preach God's word with confidence. We must evaluate our motives, measure our words, and expound the Scriptures. Simply put, that's sensible leadership.

Conclusion

# Follow-Through and Final Thoughts

IF YOU'RE FAMILIAR AT ALL WITH SPORTS, you know the importance of mechanics when it comes to performance. In particular, there's one universal step that's critical for success in every form of competition—the follow-through. Whether it's throwing a ball, shooting a basket, or swinging a bat or a club, failure to follow through will cause you to come up short every time. The same is true when it comes to our growth, both as people and as preachers. Follow-through is essential.

As preachers we all recognize the significance of applying God's word. James challenged the first-century church to avoid the self-deception of being hearers of the word without becoming doers of the word (James 1:22). His instruction echoed Jesus's challenge at the end of the Sermon on the Mount when he painted the contrast between the two builders. The wise man was anyone who "hears these words of mine and does them" while the foolish man represented one who "hears these words of mine and does not do them" (Matt. 7:24–27). The difference could not have been more drastic and the result of failing to apply the truth was catastrophic.

While we certainly wouldn't begin to compare the content of our book with Scripture, it's not uncommon for any of us to value a new lesson but fail to take the practical steps necessary to implement it in our lives and ministry. And as we all know too well, this can be true for us as preachers when we struggle to personally apply the truths of our own messages. Although failing to employ expositional leadership may not result in an immediate or complete collapse, the biblical foundation for these principles and the scriptural substance they require of our sermons does ensure that neglecting them may have serious and long-term implications for our ministries.

We trust that the biblical principles we've advocated for in this book have been practical enough to apply in your preaching. Following through, however, always requires intentionality. So we wanted to provide some final concrete suggestions that we pray will be beneficial to you. First, look at the working definition of expositional leadership that we established in the introductory chapter.

*Expositional leadership is the pastoral process of shepherding God's people through the faithful exposition of his word to conform them to the image of his Son by the power of his Spirit.*

When we first looked at this, we clarified the significance of the individual terms and phrases. Having now explored various aspects of expositional leadership throughout the book, perhaps you would revisit the definition with these elements and your particular ministry context in mind. Try parsing the definition according to the six facets of pulpit leadership discussed in their respective chapters, evaluating areas of your current preaching ministry, and exploring areas for possible growth.

For example, in the "pastoral process of shepherding God's people," are there elements of servant leadership or situational leadership that you have possibly overlooked? Are there current circumstances where it would be beneficial for you to leverage these aspects of leadership in your messages? Or in your commitment to "the faithful exposition of his word" have you missed the opportunity to address cultural issues or church dynamics that require strategic leadership? Maybe you've unintentionally neglected "the power of his Spirit" in your preparation, proclamation, or application. If so, how can you adjust your approach to sermon development and delivery to better account for this critical aspect of spiritual leadership?

Another way you might consider implementing some of these principles is by evaluating your sermons according to the different facets of expositional leadership. Instead of starting with the definition as a prompt, you can try adding a final step to your sermon preparation that looks for ways to include corporate application. You may identify related textual and theological truths that will allow you to exercise aspects of scriptural or strategic leadership for your congregation. In addition to evaluating your messages on the front end, you can also gauge the effectiveness of their leadership by watching them on video afterwards. We all know it's uncomfortable to listen to ourselves, but it can be one of the most beneficial practices for identifying areas of improvement for our delivery. Beyond recognizing ways to enhance your communication or missed leadership opportunities, you may be able to spot effective elements of expositional leadership that you're already using but previously would not have recognized. These moments of affirmation can help you become more intentional in leveraging them, or they could help you sharpen them for greater effect.

Ultimately, as we continue to grow in our pulpit ministries, our efforts to effectively unite the foundational ministry components of leadership, preaching, and shepherding must be motivated by the unified goal of glorifying Christ and sanctifying his people. The apostle Paul perfectly expressed this ultimate ambition for his preaching ministry when he wrote, "Him we proclaim, warning everyone and teaching everyone with all wisdom, that we may present everyone mature in Christ. For this I toil, struggling with all his energy that he powerfully works within me" (Col. 1:28–29).

But notice, this declaration was not only a testimony he embodied—it was a ministry philosophy that summarizes and incorporates the essential elements of expositional leadership. Scriptural leadership is the basis for his "warning everyone and teaching everyone." Spiritual leadership is only accomplished by the Holy Spirit who empowers him "with all his energy that he powerfully works within" him and transforms God's people so that they "may present everyone mature in Christ." His preaching and teaching is also characterized "with all wisdom," the divine guidance that enables him to exercise strategic and situational leadership. This wisdom and his singular commitment to preach Christ, "Him we proclaim," are the essential elements of sensible leadership. And finally, Paul exerts servant leadership through his sacrificial labor when he says, "For this I toil, struggling" on behalf of "everyone," which he does in order to achieve his desired goal.

Overall, Paul sets an excellent example for all of us in expositional leadership. May we prayerfully devote ourselves to this same end, seeing Christ glorified and his people sanctified as we proclaim him and lead his people through the faithful exposition of his word!

# General Index

# Scripture Index